Now That I'm Saved . . .

16 Ways to Experience God

Now That I'm Saved . . .

16 Ways to Experience God

Paul D. Rusnak

BRIDGE • LOGOS Publishers
South Plainfield, NJ

All Scripture quotations in this publication are taken from the King James Version of the Bible.

Now That I'm Saved . . . 16 Ways to Experience God
by Paul D. Rusnak
ISBN 0-88270-684-5
Library of Congress Catalog Card #95-77538
Copyright ©1995 by BRIDGE • LOGOS Publishers

First Printing 1996

Published by:
BRIDGE-LOGOS Publishers
2500 Hamilton Blvd.
South Plainfield, NJ 07080-2513

Printed in the United States of America.

Contents

Introduction

During the summer of 1986, I was under great conviction to align my life with the Word of God, so I spent a great deal of time in prayer. One day, just as I finished praying, I had a vision in which the Holy Spirit revealed many scriptural truths to me. This book is about those revelations and several others that God has given me since then.

The book is in two parts. The first part deals with how to pray and how to conduct spiritual warfare. The second part contains the revelations I received about God's Word. This is not, however, just another book about spiritual warfare and prayer; it's a revelation from God's Word about these subjects and many other topics that our gracious Lord has revealed to me through His Spirit and His Word.

NOW THAT I'M SAVED . . .

Like yours, my faith has been tested many times since I have been saved. The greatest test came when my daughter was in the hospital on a life-support system for five weeks. Her doctors said there was no hope for her. To get through this ordeal and be a support to our daughter, my wife and I relied fully on our faith in God and on His Word.

Our daughter was suffering a reaction to the chemotherapy treatments she had received for leukemia. We held in faith even though the hospital staff thought we were religious fanatics who were not willing to accept what—to them— was the inevitable.

It's been five years since our daughter was removed from that life-support system and she's doing great. Through that experience, my wife and I learned to live by the biblical truths about faith, prayer, and spiritual warfare. The wonderful result was that we saw a great miracle, and we continue to see miracles from God's hand every day. Jesus said that a person who has faith no greater than a grain of mustard seed would have whatever he or she asks for, and would be able to do great things for God!

> If ye have faith as a grain of mustard seed, ye shall say unto this mountain, Remove hence to yonder place; and it shall remove; and nothing shall be impossible unto you.
>
> (Matthew 17:20)

> If thou canst believe, all things are
> possible to him that believeth.
>
> (Mark 9:23)

This book was written in the hope that those who read it will gain spiritual insights into the ways of the Lord and thereby be helped and encouraged. It doesn't contain all the answers, of course, for the questions are endless—but it does provide glimpses of truth from the Word of God. It is my belief, and prayer, that if those who read this book will build on the revelations and truths it contains, they will experience the marvelous life-changing power of God's Word.

> Thy word is a lamp unto my feet, and a
> light unto my path.
>
> (Psalm 119:105)

Paul Rusnak
Charleston,
West Virginia

1

The Scarlet Covering

But I am a worm, and no man: a reproach
of men, and despised of the people.
(Psalm 22:6)

Our text verse is a prophecy that points to
Jesus on the Cross. The words, "I am a worm,"
refer to a worm-like insect found in the Middle
East.

In Psalm 22:6, the Hebrew word that is
translated as "worm" (*tola`ath*) is the same word
that is translated in many other Scriptures as
"red" or "scarlet." The word is used to describe
both the insect and the red dye made from its
dead body. It's important for us to know that
this word is used for a worm and for the red
color (dye) applied to the rams skins that were
used as a covering for the Tabernacle.[1]

There are three major types of insects that
have been used to make red dye. The one
most often used in the Middle East is an

insect that attaches itself to a leaf. Once it's attached, it stays motionless, lays its eggs, and then dies. Its body, which has formed a waxy scale over it, dries and shelters the eggs that have been deposited beneath it. When the eggs hatch, this dead body is a source of nourishment to the larvae until they are strong enough to move about. To make a red dye, the dried bodies are scraped from the leaves, ground to powder and mixed with a liquid.

Psalm 22:6 says, "I am a worm, and no man," and is clearly speaking of Jesus, comparing Him to this worm. It also says He would be "a reproach of men and despised of the people." The red-dye worm we are discussing belongs to a family of some of the most destructive insects in that part of the world. It's hated and considered a scourge. This leads us to similarities in the metaphorical comparison of Jesus with the worm: both were looked upon with disgust and hatred while they were hanging on a tree (the Cross is often referred to as a tree[2]).

The dried-up body of the worm is alluded to in Psalm 22:15: "My strength is dried up like a potsherd. . . ." The word translated "strength" in this verse means "substance." A potsherd is a piece of pottery. In the same way that the scarlet worm's lifeless and dried body covers and gives protection to the new life under it, the blood-stained body of Jesus, dried up like a piece of earthen pottery, hung from a tree and has become our covering and protection.

The red-dye worm sacrifices its life to make its body a source of life for its offspring. Jesus sacrificed His body so we, His spiritual offspring, could have life. It's the blood of Jesus that paid for our sins and presents us holy and blameless in God's sight. When the red dye made from the worm was applied to the rams' skins that covered the Tabernacle, it was a prophetic symbol of the blood of Jesus that would be applied to our earthly temples that contain our souls and spirits.[3]

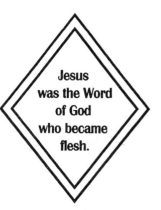

Significantly, the Hebrew word used for the worm that ate the manna is the same word used for the worm from which the red dye was made. The God-given manna of the Old Testament was symbolic of the Bread of Life (Jesus) that was to come down from heaven. The purpose of the manna was to teach God's people that they are *not* to live by bread alone, but by every Word of God (Deuteronomy 8:3 and Matthew 4:4).

Jesus was the Word of God who became flesh (John 1:14)—and as the living Word, He is the Bread of Life that came down from heaven. About Himself, He said:

3

> I am the living bread which came down
> from heaven: if any man eat of this bread, he
> shall live for ever: and the bread that I will
> give is my flesh, which I will give for the life
> of the world.
>
> (John 6:51)

The red-dye worm gives its life and flesh for its offspring; but it is not enough that the flesh is given, it must be eaten by the offspring in order for them to live. In the same way, Jesus gave His life for us, but we must eat of His flesh to live. That flesh is the Word of God. We must eat of the Word of God to live—it's the spiritual bread that gives life to our souls.

Manna became a "breeding ground" for a species of red-dye worms because of man's disobedience (Exodus 16:20), and it was because of man's disobedience that the Bread of Life— the Son of God—had to become as a worm. He was despised by the people and crucified to become the red covering for the fleshly temples of God in which we live (1 Corinthians 3:16-17). Because of this blood covering, we are made pure in the sight of God.

Speaking of His life, Jesus said:

> No man taketh it from me, but I lay it
> down of myself.
>
> (John 10:18)

Just as the scarlet worm attaches its body to the tree and dies, Jesus willingly did the same

4

for us because God loved us while we were still sinners (Romans 5:8). To be cleansed from our sins, we must receive the red covering for the temple of our bodies. To get the red dye for the ram's skin, the worm had to die. To get the red blood to cover us, Jesus had to die. Those who reject the sacrifice Jesus made to cover their sins *in this life* will never find a covering for their sins *in the next life*. Their manna-worm will never die (Mark 9:44, 46; Isaiah 66:24), and they will never have a red covering to keep them from the fires of hell. Jesus is the only way to God, and there is no other name by which we *must* be saved (John 14:6; Acts 4:12).

Through the Psalmist, the Holy Spirit uses a metaphor to show us that Jesus gave His life for us in a manner similar to the way the symbolic red-dye worm gives its life for its offspring.

[1]Exodus 26:14
[2]Galatians 3:13
[3]1 Corinthians 3:16; 6:19

2

Devices of Satan

> Lest Satan should get an advantage of us:
> for we are not ignorant of his devices.
> (2 Corinthians 2:11)

Temptations come from Satan who wants us to fail. But Christ Jesus, the living Word of God, can keep us from failing:

> For we have not an high priest which cannot be touched with the feeling of our infirmities; but was in all points tempted like as we are, yet without sin. Let us therefore come boldly unto the throne of grace, that we may obtain mercy, and find grace to help in time of need.
>
> (Hebrews 4:15-16)

Jesus was tempted with the same kind of temptations that we are, yet He never sinned. The three categories—or areas—of temptation that we all face are listed for us in 1 John 2:16—

these are the same areas in which the woman in the Garden was tempted and failed:

> For all that is in the world, the *lust of the flesh*, and the *lust of eyes*, and the *pride of life*, is not of the Father, but is of the world (italics mine).

We can go to Jesus as our High Priest who mediates with God for us[1] because He knows what it feels like to be tempted and knows the weakness of our flesh. Also, the Word of God tells us that we will not be tempted with more than we can bear (1 Corinthians 10:13).

In Luke 4:1-13, we read of how Jesus was tempted by the devil in the three areas that we are all tempted: lust of the flesh, lust of the eyes, and pride of life. These are the same areas in which the woman was tempted and failed—and in which we so often are tempted and fail—but in which Jesus did not fail.

In these passages we see Satan tempting Jesus with the lust of the flesh by encouraging Him to make bread out of stones. Jesus had fasted forty days and nights and was hungry—in fact, starvation had set in. To use His divine power to make bread was not the Father's will for Him. So Jesus used the Word of God, which is the will of God, and replied to the devil, "It is written, That man shall not live by bread alone, but by every word of God" (Luke 4:1-4).

When he could not get Jesus to fail by tempting Him with lust of the flesh, the devil tried to tempt Him with lust of the eyes. In a moment of time, he took Jesus to a high mountain and showed Him all the kingdoms of the world and said to Him, "All this power will I give thee, and the glory of them: for that is delivered unto me; and to whomsoever I will I give it. If thou therefore wilt worship me, all shall be thine." The devil was willing to trade the whole world for the souls of humanity—he wanted them all. And if he could get Jesus to fail just once, he had them. Fortunately for us, Jesus did not consider the devil's offer for one second. He used the Word of God on him again and said, "Get thee behind me, Satan: for

We will not be tempted with more than we can bear.

it is written, Thou shalt worship the Lord thy God, and him only shalt thou serve" (Luke 4:5-8).

When lust of the eyes did not work any better than lust of the flesh did, the devil tried the last area of temptation open to him: pride of life. He brought Jesus to Jerusalem and set Him on a pinnacle of the temple and said to Him, "If thou be the Son of God, cast thyself down from hence" (Luke 4:9). Satan wanted Jesus to prove He was the Son of God because he knew that if He was, the angels would protect Him. Satan knew who Jesus was, but he was trying to get

Him to prove His identity to him. But that would have ruined the task He came to earth to accomplish, which was to "destroy the works of the devil" (1 John 3:8). Pride tempts people by creating in them the egocentric desire to be noticed by others because of who they are or what they are or because of something they've done. Satan uses this very effectively among churchgoers and Christians, which are not necessarily the same. Jesus resisted the temptation of pride and resisted the devil and won by using the Word of God again. He said to the devil, "It is said, Thou shalt not tempt the Lord thy God" (Luke 4:12).

After Satan finished tempting Jesus, he departed for a season and angels came and ministered to Jesus (Luke 4:14; Matthew 4:11). Jesus' success over the devil shows the truth of what the Word says in James 4:7: "Submit yourselves therefore to God. Resist the devil, and he will flee from you." The key here is to submit yourself to God first before you try to resist—and when you do resist, don't do it in your own strength and with your own words. By faith stand in the victory of Jesus (1 John 5:4) and use the Word of God just like He did.

Satan has been a liar and deceiver (Revelation 12:9) from his first conversation with humans in the Garden of Eden. He told Eve she could disobey God and not die. We know from the account in Genesis that the man and woman experienced a spiritual death because of what happened in the Garden (see Genesis 3), and that all humanity has inherited that spiritual death from them. It's amazing that people are still falling for the same old lies of the devil—even Christians who should know better.

The temptations he used against the woman he also used against Jesus and he uses them against us—his ways haven't changed in thousands of years, we just haven't grown any smarter.

The Scripture says:

> And when the woman saw that the tree was good for food [lust of the flesh], and that it was pleasant to the eyes [lust of the eyes], and a tree to be desired to make one wise like God—[pride of life], she took of the fruit thereof, and did eat.
>
> (Genesis 3:6)

This desire to become as wise as God comes from a proud heart. Pride causes people to have too high an opinion of themselves—an exaggerated sense of self-worth and egocentric "me-ism." The serpent found pride in Eve, probed it with his words, and within Eve's heart a desire to be exalted was conceived. She wanted to be wise like God, knowing good and evil.

The Scriptures tell us that this was the condition of Lucifer's heart and was the cause of his rebellion and ultimate fall. The Holy Spirit speaking through the prophet Isaiah reports Lucifer as saying in his heart, "I will exalt my throne above the stars of God: . . . I will be like the most High" (Isaiah 14:13-14).

Any temptation Satan uses against you will fit into one of the three categories outlined by the apostle John. The acts of stealing, lying, and adultery are not the temptations. They are the result of giving in to the temptations of lust of the eyes, the pride of life, and lust of the flesh. All sins result from yielding to one of these temptations.

To help us in these vulnerable areas in which the devil will constantly probe us, we need to constantly remember and hold fast to the inspired words of the apostles Paul and Peter:

> There hath no temptation taken you but such as is common to man: but God is faithful, who will not suffer you to be tempted above that ye are able; but will with the temptation also make a way to escape, that ye may be able to bear it.
>
> (1 Corinthians 10:13)

> Submit yourselves therefore to God. Resist the devil, and he will flee from you.
>
> (James 4:7)

[1]1 Timothy 2:5; Hebrews 12:24

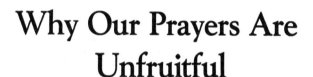

Why Our Prayers Are Unfruitful

> The thief cometh not, but for to steal, and to kill, and to destroy: I am come that they might have life, and that they might have it more abundantly.
>
> (John 10:10)

The Parable of the Sower in the fourth chapter of Mark (also Matthew 13 and John 8), illustrates the truth of John 10:10:

> Hearken; Behold, there went out a sower to sow: And it came to pass, as he sowed, some fell by the way side, and the fowls of the air came and devoured it up. And some fell on stony ground, where it had not much earth; and immediately it sprang up, because it had no depth of earth: But when the sun was up, it was scorched; and because it had no root, it withered away. And some fell among thorns, and the thorns grew up, and choked it, and it yielded no fruit. And other

> fell on good ground, and did yield fruit that sprang up and increased; and brought forth, some thirty, and some sixty, and some an hundred.
>
> (Mark 4:3-8)

Jesus' disciples did not understand this parable, so when they were alone He explained it to them:

> And he said unto them, Know ye not this parable? and how then will ye know all parables? The sower soweth the word. And these are they by the way side, where the word is sown; but when they have heard, Satan cometh immediately, and taketh away the word that was sown in their hearts.
>
> (Mark 4:13-16)

These are the people who never understand the Word of God. Satan steals it out of their hearts and blinds them to the gospel: "In whom the god of this world hath blinded the minds of them which believe not, lest the light of the glorious gospel of Christ, who is the image of God, should shine unto them" (2 Corinthians 4:4; see also Matthew 13:19).

To receive what is in the Word and make it part of our lives, we must understand what it says and keep it in our hearts— hide it deep and solid within us so Satan can't find it and dislodge it from us. There's a good spiritual reason for doing this, as the Psalmist tells us: "Thy word have I hid in mine heart, that I might not sin against thee" (Psalm 119:11).

Satan not only directly steals the Word out of the hearts of those who hear the gospel, he also does it by bringing things against them that cause them to stumble and fall away.

And these are they likewise which are sown on stony ground; who, when they have heard the word, immediately receive it with gladness; And have no root in themselves, and so endure but for a time: afterward, when affliction or persecution ariseth for the word's sake, immediately they are offended.

(Mark 4:16-17)

Satan can't steal the Word that's in our hearts.

Afflictions or persecutions rise like the midday sun, and under the heat of the trials this group of people wither like plants with weak root systems. They spiritually wither up and die when the trials come because the Word has not been able to take root in their hearts. They cannot take the heat of the afflictions or persecutions and they lose their faith and fall away (Luke 21:26).

There is also a group that doesn't fall away but never accomplishes anything for the kingdom of God, as Jesus tells us:

> And these are they which are sown among thorns; such as hear the word, And the cares of this world, and the deceitfulness of riches, and lusts of other things entering in, choke the word, and it becometh unfruitful.
>
> (Mark 4:18-19)

If Satan can't steal the Word that's in our hearts, or kill our faith in God and His Word, he will try to keep us from producing fruit by polluting the ground where the Word has been sown—our hearts. To do this, he uses the cares of this world, the deceitfulness of riches, and lust for other things—those areas of temptation that we discussed before (1 John 2:16).

If Satan can pollute our hearts with those things, we will not produce any fruit. Not only does Satan use the world's pleasures—lusts and deceitfulness of riches—he also uses situations and circumstances in his effort to make us unfruitful.

The more we get involved with things of this world, the more we want and gather to ourselves those things the world covets and considers important, the less productive the Word will become in our lives. This is especially true in our prayer-life—the more the things of the world crowd into our hearts, the less effective are our prayers, and the less often we pray.

Jesus came that we might have life—*zôê*, the life that God has in Himself—and that we might have it "more abundantly;" that is, increasingly have more of it. This increasing life of God is what Peter was referring to when he wrote, "Whereby are given unto us exceeding great and precious promises: that by these ye might be *partakers of the divine nature,* having escaped the corruption that is in the world through lust" (2 Peter 1:4—italics mine). It's also what the writer of the Book of Hebrews was referring to when he wrote, "For they verily for a few days chastened us after their own pleasure; but he for our profit, that we might be *partakers of his holiness.* (Hebrews 12:10—italics mine).

Some of the greatest men and women of God were thrown into prison and executed for their faith, like John the Baptist and the apostles James and Paul—John was the only apostle who wasn't put to death for his faith. But what an abundant life they had in Christ; how filled they were with the Spirit of God; how the divine life, the *zôê* life of God, poured out of them to others! They fought the good fight, they kept the faith, and they inspired faith in millions of others. Someone once wrote, "The seed of the gospel of Jesus Christ has been watered by the blood of Christian martyrs." These great saints of God were not involved with storing up treasures on earth where moth and rust corrupt, they were focused on laying up treasures in heaven, on storing up souls for their Lord, Jesus Christ (Matthew 6:19-21).

These faithful men and women are among the ones Jesus referred to when He said the Word fell on good ground—in an honest and good heart. These are the folks who heard the Word, kept it, and brought forth fruit with patience (Luke 8:15).

It is the same when we pray; the fruit of our prayers must be brought forth with faith, patience, and persistence. It was after Abraham patiently endured that he received the promise (Hebrews 6:15 and 11:8). By not losing faith and by patiently and persistently waiting, the promise was made sure. This is also the principle behind Jesus' parables about the friend in Luke 11:5-8, and the unjust judge in Luke 18:1-8.

The writer of Hebrews urges each of us to be diligent to hold fast in this same kind of patient and persistent faith:

> We want each of you to show this same diligence to the very end, in order to make your hope sure. We do not want you to become lazy, but to imitate those who through faith and patience inherit what has been promised.
>
> (Hebrews 6:11-12, NIV)

We must be diligent until we receive our promise. We must not give up hope until the answer comes. Abraham endured because God's Word was sown in the good ground of his heart. He believed God's promise and doubt did not enter his heart to choke the Word. But like a lot of us, even though he didn't doubt that he would receive the promise, he got into trouble by trying to make it come about in his own way—and thus he produced Ishmael, who was not the heir God promised.

Although we may hold onto God's promise and produce fruit, we can still do things that will cause us to produce less than 100 percent. That's why the Lord said that some produced thirty fold (30%), some sixty (60%), and some a hundred (100%). It's the 100% production of Mark 4:20 that all of us should strive for: "And these are they which are sown on good ground; such as hear the word, and receive it, and bring forth fruit, some thirtyfold, some sixty, and some an hundred." Let's not be partial producers, let's produce all that Christ died to give us and that God has for us.

When we're waiting for an answer to our prayers, we are actually waiting for the fulfillment of one or more of God's promises. The answer will come, but most of the time it will come only after we have patiently endured in the same way Abraham did. The reason why most of our prayers never bring forth fruit is that while we're waiting for the promise, Satan buffets us so we'll grow weary and begin to doubt. He's constantly trying to steal the Word out of our hearts, trying to kill our faith in God's Word, and trying to destroy our ability to produce fruit from the Word that is sown in our hearts.

NOW THAT I'M SAVED...

God cannot lie because His power is so great that whatever He says happens! If He promises us something in His Word, it is ours. If we ask for something according to a promise from His Word, and we have an honest and a good heart, and if we keep the Word securely in our hearts, the fruit of our prayers will be brought forth with patience. If we patiently wait, no matter what comes our way, the promise will come. If we accept less than what we ask for, we will get less. Also, if we expect less than what we ask for because we doubt in our hearts, we will also receive less. Always remember, if you receive less than what God promised, you've been robbed by your enemy, Satan.

God won't give us a stone if we ask for bread. So if I ask for bread and start to get a stone, should I accept it? Who would the stone be from? Don't accept the enemy's counterfeit gifts. God cannot lie because He's God, and anything less than what you asked for—if you asked according to His Word—is not what He promised. Sometimes the answer comes in parts. If it does, keep enduring patiently while waiting for *all* of the answer.

Remember, the children of Israel had to possess the Promised Land one step at a time. Have the same diligence as those who, through faith and patience, inherited what was promised. Don't be afraid. Only believe. We begin to fear when we don't totally trust in God and truly believe His promises. If we truly believe, we will trust Him, and we will not be afraid. With our hearts filled with faith, there is no room for doubt, discouragement, or fear. Always keep in mind who He is that you are having faith in: GOD!

4

The Name of Jesus

> I am the vine, ye are the branches. He that abideth in me, and I in him, the same bringeth forth much fruit: for without me ye can do nothing. If ye abide in me, and my words abide in you, ye shall ask what ye will, and it shall be done unto you.
>
> (John 15:5, 7)

We abide in Christ and in His love by keeping His commandments, as we are told in John 15:10 and 1 John 2:3-6. We are also told in John 14:13 and 16:23-24 that we are to ask in Jesus' name, and whatever we ask for will happen or we will receive. But none of these are effective if we don't have the catalyst to prayer abiding in our hearts—that catalyst is His Word. That's why we must not let the enemy steal the Word or destroy its ability to produce fruit in our lives. By that combination of abiding in His Word, obeying His commandments, and using

His name, Christ Jesus has given us the greatest power in the world. This all seems very simple but not easy. If it was easy, there would be more answers to prayers in the Church today. The reason the Church does not have the prayer power it once had is that the leaven of the Pharisees and Sadducees—religious skepticism and unbelief—has been mixed with our faith. Because we don't have the power, we justify our lack of power by watering down the Word of God. Many have chosen to believe that supernatural power was either for the early Church, or that they don't have to obey God's Word and bring forth the fruit and prayer results that Jesus told us to.

God does not change and He cannot lie. If He promises something, He keeps His promise. If we aren't receiving what God has promised, the problem is on our end. Many display spiritual gifts, but not many have power-packed prayer lives. I'm not referring to nice-sounding prayers or long prayers. I'm talking about seeing the answers come from heaven. If we were as spiritual as we need to be, we would see the fruit of our prayers coming forth. We'll never see them until we're truly abiding in Him and His Word is abiding in us. If His Word is truly abiding in us, we won't doubt and we'll keep His commandments.

Many believe they don't have to keep His commandments in order to abide in Him. That's a lie and many have died unprepared by believing this deception. This is a good example of how the leaven of the Pharisees and Sadducees has entered into the teachings of many. It doesn't matter if you, I, or anyone else believe that we don't have to keep His commandments, God's Word says that we must.

In Matthew 17:20, Jesus said that if we had faith like a mustard seed we could say to a mountain, "remove hence to yonder place," and it would be removed. Then Jesus tells us, "Nothing shall be impossible unto you." Mustard-seed faith doesn't sound like much faith, but by having even this much there is no room left for doubt in our hearts.

He keeps His promise.

> Verily I say unto you, If ye have faith, and doubt not, ye shall not only do this which is done to the fig tree, but also if ye shall say unto this mountain, Be thou removed, and be thou cast into the sea; it shall be done. And all things, whatsoever ye shall ask in prayer, believing, ye shall receive.
>
> (Matthew 21:21-22)

The key is not to doubt—to simply believe. If you're going to doubt anything, doubt your doubts—they're not trustworthy. Only the Word of God is!

We either have faith or we don't. If we have any doubt in our hearts, we don't have faith the size of a mustard seed. If we don't doubt in our hearts, then it stands to reason that we at least have faith the size of a mustard seed! Truly, that is all we need.

> Without faith it is impossible to please him: for he that cometh to God must believe that he is, and that he is the rewarder of them that diligently seek him.

(Hebrews 11:6)

Praying in Faith

> After this manner therefore pray ye
> (Matthew 6:9)

This model prayer of Jesus, known as the Lord's Prayer, provides us with an outline, or framework, on which to build a faith-life of prayer:

> Our Father which art in heaven—*Call upon Him.*

(Matthew 6:9)

> Hallowed be thy name—*Praise Him.*
> (Matthew 6:9)

> Thy kingdom come. Thy will be done in earth, as it is in heaven—*Submit to His will.*
> (Matthew 6:10)

Give us this day our daily bread—*Ask for His help.*

(Matthew 6:11)

And forgive us our debts, as we forgive our debtors—*Ask for forgiveness with a forgiving heart.*

(Matthew 6:12)

And lead us not into temptation—*Ask for guidance.*

(Matthew 6:13)

But deliver us from evil—*Ask for deliverance from evil.*

(Matthew 6:13)

For thine is the kingdom, and the power, and the glory for ever—*Praise Him.*

(Matthew 6:13)

Amen—So be it—*Believe Him*

(Matthew 6:13)

Most important: Ask in Jesus' name. Jesus is the mediator between God and man.

And whatsoever ye shall ask in my name, that will I do, that the Father may be glorified in the Son.

(John 14:13)

Let your requests be made to God with thanks-giving. Thanksgiving is a part of praise, and praise is a part of prayer. In Philippians 4:6

we read: "Be careful for nothing: but in every thing by prayer and supplication with thanksgiving let your requests be made known unto God."

This is a step-by-step illustration of how to pray in faith using the example Jesus gave us. At first, you can use the above outline. As you think of the words, "Our Father which art in heaven," call upon Him. Then go to the next step, following the example Jesus gave us.

Since your needs will change from day to day, when you ask for your daily needs, ask for what you need on that particular day. Also keep in mind that because we must live by more than bread alone, our souls need the spiritual bread found in God's Word. When you pray, therefore, ask God for revelation of the Word that you will read that day. Only when we understand His Word does it feed our souls—and revelation comes by the Holy Spirit explaining the meaning of the Scriptures to us.

God only hears prayers that are asked according to His will (John 5:14-15). Whatever we ask for we will receive from Him because we keep His commandments, and do those things that are pleasing in His sight (1 John 3:22). Remember, God doesn't hear us because of much speaking; He looks at our hearts. He also knows what we need before we ask so that we acknowledge our dependence upon Him and exercise our faith. Also, when we ask, we must do so in steadfast faith and not waver between faith and unbelief, for if we waver we will get nothing (James 1:6-7).

This eleven-step prayer outline, based on the model prayer of Jesus and other Scriptures, is only an example of how to pray in faith. Prayer must not become a formality; it must come from the heart—for the only faith-prayer that works is the one that comes out of the heart's faith (Mark 11:23).

However, because the Lord's Prayer is a model that Jesus gave His disciples when they asked Him to teach them to pray, our prayers need to include the components He outlined.

> Rejoice evermore. Pray without ceasing.
> In every thing give thanks: for this is the will
> of God in Christ Jesus concerning you.
> (1 Thessalonians 5:16-18)

5

How to Fight the Good Fight of Faith

I have fought a good fight, I have
finished my course, I have kept the faith.
(2 Timothy 4:7)

The apostle Paul tells us in Ephesians 6:4, that we must have our loins "girt about with truth." 1 Peter 1:13 helps us to understand that Paul is referring to the loins of the mind. Our minds must be girt about with truth. Both Paul and Peter were speaking of the same thing. Paul was using the illustration of a warrior to show that in spiritual warfare the loins of our mind must be girt about with truth. This truth is the Word of God—John 17:17: "Sanctify them through thy truth: thy word is truth," and Ephesians 1:13: " . . .the word of truth, the gospel of your salvation."

Next, we must have on the breastplate of righteousnes. 1 Thessalonians 5:8 tells us that this breastplate is made of faith and love: "But let us, who are of the day, be sober, putting on the breastplate of faith and love."

Our faith must be in His Word, and we must have the love of Christ in our hearts. If we love Him, we will keep His commandments. Jesus said:

> By this shall all men know that ye are my disciples, if we have love one to another.
> (John 13:35)

We must have our feet shod with the preparation of the gospel of peace. We must follow Him and do what His Word says. If we do, we will be prepared when the battle comes.

We must be wearing the shield of faith that will quench all the fiery darts of the wicked. This shield of faith comes from a knowledge of God's Word, for it is faith in God's Word that will keep us from all the fiery darts of the wicked.

We must also have on the helmet of salvation. We know from 1 Thessalonians 5:8 that this helmet is the hope of salvation: ". . . and for an helmet, the hope of salvation." Our hope is in God's Word and in His promise of our salvation. Our hope must be built upon the promises found in God's Word. Hope of salvation will keep us encouraged even in the darkest of places. Hebrews 6:19 tells us that this hope "we have as an anchor of the soul."

The truth of God's Word guards our minds as we prepare to resist the devil. When the enemy tries to kill, steal, or destroy our faith, we can stand against him only to the degree that our thoughts are protected by God's Word.

The Word of God is also a breastplate that protects our hearts with faith and love. It is a guide to direct the paths of our feet. When our faith is in the Word, the Word becomes our shield that protects us from all the fiery darts of the wicked one.

God's Word is our hope of salvation and a sword against which all the powers of darkness must yield. As long as we abide in Christ, and His Word abides in us, we'll be able to stand against all the devices of Satan. It is our faith in the Word of God that will bind the powers of darkness. There is no greater power that God has given to us than claiming the promises of His Word, in the name of Jesus. If we are submitted to God, have the whole armor of God in place, and pray in faith without wavering, we will successfully bring down the strongholds of the enemy.

Each day, after we have made sure that we have the whole armor of God on, we are ready to do battle. In Ephesians 6:18, after Paul tells us to put on the full armor of God, he says to pray, "always with all prayer and supplication [*earnestness*] in the Spirit." James 4:7 says:

> Submit yourselves therefore to God.
> Resist the devil, and he will flee from you.

Notice that he says first to submit ourselves to God. This is essential and it must take place before we'll be able to resist the devil. If we don't first submit ourselves to God, Satan will sift us like wheat.

The Greek word *antiassomai*, translated as "resist" in James 4:7, is the same word that is translated as "withstand" in Ephesians 6:13. James tells us to submit ourselves to God and then, when we resist the devil, he will flee from us. In Ephesians 6:10-18, Paul tells us that we resist the devil by having on the armor of God; then he tells us to pray.

When we come against the powers of darkness in prayer while we are dressed in the full armor of God, we are able to stand against the devil's devices and make him flee from us.

If we pray according to God's will, we will not ask amiss for things which would be foolish. We must ask according to His will, and ask in faith, while abiding in Christ:

> And this is the confidence that we have in him, that, if we ask anything according to his will, he heareth us: And if we know that he hear us, whatsoever we ask, we know that we have the petitions that we desire of him.
>
> (1 John 5:14-15)

But we must be sure not to have any doubt in our hearts. James says we must ask in faith; nothing wavering:

> For he that wavereth is like a wave of the sea driven with the wind and tossed. For let not that man think he shall receive any thing of the Lord.
>
> (James 1:6-7)

We need to put on every piece of the armor of God daily. This is done by having God's love and His Word abiding in our hearts. If we abide in Him, putting our faith in His Word, and if we do not waver, He will not fail us. In the same way that the body is dead without the spirit, and faith is dead without works, prayer without faith is also dead.

Remember, before Satan could take what God had given to Adam and Eve in the Garden, he had to first rob them of their faith in God's Word. The same is true with us; if we keep our faith in God's Word and obey what it says, we will stand. The kingdom of God on earth operates by faith. We receive the promises that God gives to us by faith.

Spiritual warfare is a battle of faith. If the enemy can steal our faith in God's Word, he will have no problem in taking what is ours. Be not afraid; only believe; put on the whole armor of God, and in the name of Jesus, take from the enemy what is yours.

While fighting the powers of darkness and keeping the faith, keep your eyes on Jesus. Don't look at others who have suffered losses and judge them. If someone has suffered a loss, comfort that person. We are called to believe God, not to judge. I say this because I've often seen someone looking at another who has suffered, then saying, "It's because they didn't have enough faith."

That would be like me going up to the apostle Paul and saying, "The reason you have a thorn in your flesh, and have suffered so much affliction, is because you don't have enough faith!" This would be as foolish for me to do as it would be for a Christian to look at a fellow believer and say the same thing. I encourage you not to look at others and judge; just believe. We are not called to judge, we are called to believe. Remember, in order to have faith in our hearts, there must be no doubt whatsoever.

> He that cometh to God must believe that he is, and that he is a rewarder of them that diligently seek him.
>
> (Hebrews 11:6)

Daniel's Fight of Faith

> And, behold, an hand touched me, which set me upon my knees and upon the palms of my hands. And he said unto me, O Daniel, a man greatly beloved, understand the words that I speak unto thee, and stand upright: for unto thee am I now sent. And

when he had spoken this word unto me, I stood trembling. Then he said unto me, Fear not, Daniel: for from the first day that thou didst set thine heart to understand, and to chasten thyself before thy God, thy words were heard, and I am come for thy words. But the prince of the kingdom of Persia withstood me one and twenty days: but, lo, Michael, one of the chief princes, came to help me; and I remained there with the kings of Persia. Now I am come to make thee understand what shall befall thy people in the latter days: for yet the vision is for many days.

(Daniel 10:10-14)

It took Daniel many days before he received an answer to his prayer. God sent the answer the first day Daniel had asked, but it was held up by the powers of darkness. Every time an answer is late in coming, however, it may not be for this reason. Whatever the reason is, we must do as Daniel did and keep on praying and believing until it comes. If God has heard you, then He has given you what you ask for—the key to receiving it is to hold on until it comes.

As sure as our Savior lives, if we ask with faith in His Word—if we obey Him and do what pleases Him—He will give us what we ask of Him. If God has heard us, which He has if we do these things, we also know that He has given us what we have asked Him for (1 John 5:14-15). If we have not received the answer, it's because it has been delayed for some reason.

Just because we haven't received what we've asked for doesn't necessarily mean God hasn't sent the promise. This was true in the story of Daniel. If we haven't received what we've asked for, we must not let doubt enter our hearts. The reason Daniel got his answer is that he never gave up—he persisted until he got what he had asked for.

There are times when we have to put on the full armor of God, and in prayer, without doubting, take from the enemy what God has given to us. If God has given something to us, we have a right to lay claim to it, and using our spiritual weapons, to take it by force. Remember, the children of Israel had to take the Promised Land one step at a time. God would never have given us spiritual armor if we didn't have to do battle.

This may sound strange, but this is how the kingdom of God operates on this planet. The kingdom of God suffers violence, and we must possess it by force. This is why God has given us mighty weapons to pull down the enemy's strongholds. Satan has come to steal, kill, and destroy. But God has given us all we need to defeat the powers of darkness. We are in a war, and our lives, and the lives of our loved ones, are at stake. Before we can be assured of victory, we must be prepared. To be prepared, we must have on the whole armor of God. Then we must pray with faith, never doubting God's Word or His ability.

No matter what things look like, believe God's Word and keep on praying. Keep in mind that "it isn't over until it's over." If you lose a battle, pick yourself up and keep pressing on—be determined, be persistent, and keep on keeping on. But until it's over, keep believing and don't accept less than what God has promised you. The only way for Satan to win is for you to lose your faith and start doubting. Satan tries to rob you of what is yours. He can do this only if you let him. As I said before, even in the Garden, the serpent had to first destroy the faith of Adam and Eve in God's Word before he could take what God had given them.

If we believe God has given us what we've asked for and we haven't received it, we have a right to demand that the powers of darkness let it loose. The powers of darkness build up strongholds and we must tear them down, using the mighty spiritual weapons God has given to us.

This is what God showed me, and I have lived by it and have seen His power move and bring forth a great miracle. Many times we must wait upon the Lord, but sometimes we need help right now. There are certain situations in which we have a right to go before the throne of God and demand the release of what is rightfully ours. We don't demand of God, for we're not, nor will we ever be, in a position to demand anything of God. But the Bible tells us that Satan accuses us day and night before God.

NOW THAT I'M SAVED. . .

If I am going to take on the powers of darkness, and even defy Satan himself, I am going to do it while I am before the throne of God in prayer.

First, we make our petition known. Next, we plead our case to the Father and let Jesus intercede for us. To have great faith, we must not have any doubt in our hearts. If we truly believe, we will neither expect less, nor accept less, than what God has promised. God cannot lie!

If we believe 1 John 5:14-15, we can go before God with confidence that we are entitled to what He has already given to us. The only way we can have the faith we need, is to put our faith in God's Word. We must also understand that we don't receive from God because we deserve it—it is only by God's grace, His promises, and the blood of Jesus that we are entitled to receive anything. When we take our petitions before God, we must take the promises of His Word as our evidence that we are entitled to receive them. We must also look to His righteousness, never to our own. A trick of Satan is to get us to look to our own worthiness. If we do this, doubt will enter our hearts and we will be robbed of what is ours.We have a right to what God has promised us, not because we are worthy within ourselves, but because of the work Jesus accomplished on the Cross, and because of God's grace. God has given us many promises and we must not let Satan steal them by stealing the Word out of our hearts, by killing our faith in God's Word, or by destroying the ability of the

Word to bring forth fruit by polluting the ground where it is sown.

We must lay hold of what God has promised us by faith, using God's armor to fight the powers of darkness that seek to steal what God has given us.

.

6

Trials of Faith for the Glory of God

> There was a man in the land of Uz, whose name was Job; and that man was perfect and upright, and one that feared God.
>
> (Job 1:1)

When God asked Satan where he had been, the devil replied, "From going to and fro in the earth" (Job 1:7). The apostle Peter tells us that Satan still walks about, seeking whom he may devour (1 Peter 5:8). So the story of Job and the things we can learn from it are very important to us.

Satan accused Job of serving God because of the wealth and protection God had given to him. Satan said that if God took away what Job had, Job would curse Him. We know from the account in the Bible that Job, by being faithful, proved Satan to be a liar. God allowed Satan to try Job to disprove Satan's accusation of Job, and so that He would be glorified by Job's faithfulness.

Does Satan still accuse God's children in the same way he accused Job? In Revelation 12:10, the Word says that Satan is "the accuser of our brethren," day and night before God. Some people believe that Satan no longer has the access that would enable him to do this, but this is not so.

One day while I was in prayer, I asked God why I was going through the trials I was experiencing at that time. Had I done something that was not pleasing to Him? I was surprised when God answered, "Do you remember the story of Job? He went through his trials for the glory of God." This direct word from God to me helped me immensely in my trials.

Not all of Satan's accusations are false. Every time one of God's children falls or gives in to temptation, Satan proves himself to be right. How we react to trials not only affects our earthly situation, it also affects things in heaven. Whether God is glorified, or Satan, depends on our actions.

Many times we wonder why we have to go through trials. We can't understand why God allows us to suffer. One reason we do, as revealed in the Word of God, is that many times we are permitted to go through them for the same reason Job had to face them—so God can be glorified.

Job was allowed to go through his trials, not just to see how much he could take, but so God would be glorified by his faithfulness. Because Job was faithful, God received the glory. If Job had not been faithful, Satan would have said, "I told you he was serving you just for what you had given him," and then Satan would have received the glory.

If we are not patient, holding onto our faith in God while we are facing trials, God will not receive any glory. All the glory, in such a case, will go to Satan. However, when we go through the fire in the same way that Shadrach, Meshach, and Abednego did (Daniel 3:19-30), God will be glorified.

God never changes!

When we walk by faith, we must continually remind ourselves from where we have come, and with thanksgiving never forget the trials God has brought us through. By doing this, we will not fail to remember how faithful God is to help us in our most urgent times of need. Because God never changes, we know that what He did for us in the past He will do for us in the future. Having this knowledge will enable us to turn our faces directly into the fury of the storm and press on. Our confidence will be rooted in the certainty that He is with us in the storms that rage around us.

> And the Lord shall help them, and deliver
> them: he shall deliver them from the wicked,
> and save them, because they trust in him.
>
> (Psalm 37:40)

Trials Perfect Our Faith

> Blessed is the man that endureth
> temptation: for when he is tried, he shall
> receive the crown of life, which the Lord hath
> promised to them that love him.
>
> (James 1:12)

Trials are beneficial to us, if we endure them faithfully. When we endure trials and trust in God, we learn patience. By patiently enduring our trials, our faith is increased as we gain experience, and God is glorified by our faithfulness.

> But without faith it is impossible to please
> him [God].
>
> (Hebrews 11:6)

God isn't glorified when we don't serve Him in faith. That's one reason why faith is so important. When we complain and murmur as we go through trials; when we fuss and fume about what's happening to us, we're not walking in faith. We're walking in unbelief and lack of trust and confidence in God. So our faith isn't purified and strengthened by the test and God isn't glorified. We don't do what the apostle Peter exhorted the disciples to do:

> Wherein ye greatly rejoice, though now for
> a season, if need be, ye are in heaviness
> through manifold temptations: That the trial
> of your faith, being much more precious than
> of gold that perisheth, though it be tried with
> fire, might be found unto praise and honour
> and glory at the appearing of Jesus Christ.
> (1 Peter 1:6-7)

The children of Israel got into trouble as a result of their murmuring and complaining against Moses and Aaron. Their complaints were not just directed at their leaders but also against God. This should be a lesson to those who murmur and complain against those God has put in authority over them (Exodus 15-17)!

If we have total trust in God, we won't worry and all murmuring and complaining will be gone from our lives. It's only through patiently enduring our trials that we learn to trust God. Whenever we take the time to look back, we can see that He is able to deliver us now because He has delivered us before. It wasn't until after Job patiently endured his trials that he saw, with his eyes, the faithfulness of God revealed. Before that, he had to go by only what he heard (Job 42:5). Only when faith is allowed to complete its work, can we see how faithful and able God is to deliver us. Keep this in mind, wait upon God, and see His salvation. We receive the promises of God by patiently waiting for them (Hebrews 6:12 and 10:36).

Remember, in the same way that God was with Shadrach, Meshach, and Abednego, and with Job, He is with you every step. He will never leave you or forsake you. When you are required to go through trials by fire, don't let Satan rob you of your reward, and rob God of the glory which is rightfully His. Be faithful, trust God, and be content with what you have.

> Let your light so shine before men, that they may see your good works, and glorify your Father which is in heaven.
> (Matthew 5:16)

If we are to shine as lights in the world, we must not murmur and complain. A light shines brightest when it's in the darkest place. Conversely, worry breeds murmuring and complaining. When worry has done its work, it produces fear, and our faith is destroyed. But when we keep our eyes on God and patiently endure our trials, it gives us hope, because by such endurance we can see the faith-fulness of God revealed in our lives. As long as we have hope, we have victory over fear.

To have faith in God, we must trust Him, and in order to learn to trust Him, we must have patience. Only through patience do we learn to trust God. The more our trust grows, the more our faith will grow; the greater our faith is, the more patience we will have. One thing is certain, we'll never have great faith until we learn to patiently endure our trials without murmuring, complaining, or worrying. Great faith is totally trusting God and having no doubt, no matter how bad things may seem.

> Trust in the Lord with all thine heart; and lean not unto thine own understanding. In all thy ways acknowledge him, and he shall direct thy paths.
>
> (Proverbs 3:5-6)

We either have faith or we don't. When Jesus was asked by His disciples why the demon would not come out of a certain man's son, He told them it was because of their unbelief. He also told them that if they had faith as a grain of mustard seed, they could order a mountain to move from one place to another, and it would obey them. In fact, He said, "Nothing shall be impossible unto you" (Matthew 17:20).

The key to having great faith is not doubting God's Word or His ability. Because the disciples had doubt in their hearts, they didn't even have a mustard seed of faith. If we run into this kind of problem—one in which we don't have faith enough to overcome—we must fast and pray. When Jesus said, "This kind can come forth by nothing, but by prayer and fasting" (Mark 9:29), He was referring to the kind of situation in which we don't have faith enough to overcome it. He had just told them the reason they could not cast the deaf and dumb spirit out of the child was that they had doubt. If they would have had faith equivalent to a mustard seed, nothing would have been impossible to them. If they had not doubted, they would have been able to cast the evil spirit out of the boy.

God is glorified when we are faithful and obedient. In John 17:4, Jesus said to the Father:

> I have glorified thee on the earth: I have finished the work thou gavest me to do.

The same verse in the New International Version reads:

> I have brought you glory on earth by completing the work you gave me to do.

We glorify God by our works and by our faithfulness, and when this happens, He is glorified not only on earth but also in heaven.

7

The Light of the World

When we are obedient to God's word and walk in the light, people will see our good works and God will be glorified (Matthew 5:16). The Bible says if we walk in the light as He is in the light, the blood of Jesus cleanses us from all sin (1 John 1:6-7). People are led out of darkness and into the light by hearing the word of God and by the testimony we give as we walk in obedience. In the Old Testament, God spoke through His prophets and the people had a witness of His presence by the light that shined from the breastplate originally worn by Aaron. The following study shows how this breastplate is related to Jesus Christ, the Light of the world.

Although the words *urim* and *thummim* are not used in the Old Testament except in reference to the objects in the breastplate of the priests garment, we can find clues to what these words mean by looking at their singular meaning. Both of these words are plural for singular words. This tells us that concerning the objects, *urim* and *thummim*, there were more than one of each object.

The Greek word *uwriym* translated *urim* is plural for the word *urw* which means "flame," and is translated "fire" and "light" in the King James Version. *Urw* was also used in reference to the light produced by a fire (Isaiah 50:4, "walk in the "light" of your fire.") The word *urw* comes from the word *owr* which means to make luminous. If someone was speaking of just one of the *urim*, they would have used the word *urw* (some reference books translate this word *ur*).

There are two types of precious stones and the word *urim* was used as a name of one of the two types placed in the breastplate. The stones referred to as *urim*, were the ones which are transparent and cut with several small flat surfaces so they will have a brilliance. Today these stones are referred to as "faceted" or "brilliant." The word *uwr* or its plural *uwriym*, translated *urim*, was in reference to these type of stones because of their brilliance.

The stones referred to as *thummim*, were those that we call "opaque." Light will not penetrate these stones because they're not transparent. They are cut in a convex, (curved or rounded like the exterior of a sphere or circle). These stones are highly polished and are not faceted. They were referred to as *thummim* because they were cut in the manner described above. The singular word for the word translated *thummim* means "perfection." A gem cut in this manner today is known as "cabochon."

The Jewish historian Josephus, stated in his writings, *Antiquities Of The Jews,* book 3, chapters 7 and 8, that the twelve stones were extraordinary in largeness and beauty. He also said, "God declared beforehand, by those twelve stones which the high priest bare on his breast, and which were inserted into his breastplate, when they should be victorious in battle; for so great a splendor shone forth from them before the army began to march, that all the people were sensible of God's being present for their assistance."

This is the most reliable reference outside of the Bible I have found to support my belief, that the *urim* and *thummim* were nothing other than the two type of stones placed in the breastplate. I believe the writings of the historian Josephus, are more creditable than the opposing view of anyone else who would only be guessing. I also discussed this view with a gemologist, and he agreed that these words were very likely used in relation to the two type of stones (the "lights" and "perfections").

Nowhere in the Bible does it speak of the stones, and the *urim* and *thummim* together, as being two separate items. This is because when it refers to the *urim* and *thummim*, it is speaking of the two type of stones—the "lights" and the "perfections." One thing is for sure, the *urim* and *thummim* were not some mysterious objects that were not included in the description of the priestly garments. The description given in the Bible is detailed and accurate.

Josephus said the breastplate and the sardonyx (one of the stones on the priest's shoulder) quit shining two hundred years before he wrote his book, because God was displeased at their transgressions of His law. This would have been at least a hundred and fifty years before the Crucifixion. This means that the nation of Israel had no light to guide them for many generations. Understanding this, we can see the relationship of Christ being the light of the world, and them being in darkness without the light that came from the breastplate   (which was symbolic of the spiritual darkness they were in).

In John 1:4, where the life in Jesus is referred to as "the light of men," the Greek word translated "light" means "to shine or make manifest, especially by rays." I can clearly see the relation between the light that came from the stones in the breastplate and the light that was in Jesus. The breastplate is not around to shine forth the light so people can see God is with them. But Jesus said that we are the light of the world (Matthew 5:14-16). This is because the life that is in Jesus is now in us. Because of this, just as the people saw the light shine forth from the stones in the breastplate, people can see the light shine forth from our hearts, and be aware of the presence of God.

When the light quit coming from the stones, it was an indication that God's presence was no longer among them. Is it not also an indication His presence is not with us if our light never shines, so that people around us are made aware of His presence? Jesus said, "Ye are the light of the world. A city set on a hill cannot be hid. Neither do men light a candle, and put it under a bushel, but on a candlestick; and it giveth light unto all that are in the house. Let your light so shine before men that they may see your good works, and glorify your Father which is in heaven" (Matthew 5:14-16).

We can see by this Scripture that when our light shines, it can be seen by others, and what they see is our good works. If our light is to shine, we must do the things God's Word tells us to do. We must become servants and help those in need without expecting something in return. We must love our neighbor as we love ourselves, strive to live as peaceful as possible with all people, hold no grudge in our heart, and obey the commandments of our God; expecting no reward from men and women, but looking to our God who shall reward us at His coming (Matthew 16:27). We must be witnesses, not in word only, but also in deed!

The Light of the Anointing That Abides in Us

> But the anointing which ye have received
> of him abideth in you.
>
> (1 John 2:27)

The anointing is extremely important to us. It can be compared to an oil-burning lamp. In the Scriptures, oil is symbolic of the Holy Spirit. So the anointing that John speaks of as abiding in us is the Holy Spirit—He is the anointing that we have received from God. We could therefore say that "on-fire Christians" are those in whom the oil that is God's Spirit has been ignited within them and is a roaring flame. It is that flame within us that radiates forth Christ and makes us the lights of the world. But to burn brightly and truly show Christ, we often have to have our "wicks trimmed."

The lamp wick is like our wills. In the same way that the charred, unusable part of a lamp's wick must be cut off, or trimmed, in order to enable the lamp to give off maximum light, so must our "self-will" (carnal nature) be trimmed. The cutting away of the wick is symbolic of the dying out to our carnal nature. This needs to happen because our carnal nature is enmity (hostility) against God (Romans 8:7 and James 4:4).

Differing intensities of light are produced, depending on how much oil we have within us, and depending on the condition of our wick. The purpose of the anointing is to reflect the light of Jesus Christ and to bring those who are in darkness into the light. Only when we reflect the light of Christ can those in the world see that they are lost in total darkness. When they see this, they have a choice—either to stay in darkness or to come into the glorious light of the gospel of Christ, and thereby be saved.

Changed Into His Image

> But we all, with open face beholding as in a glass the glory of the Lord, are changed into the same image from glory to glory, even as by the Spirit of the Lord.
>
> (2 Corinthians 3:18)

Moses spent forty days and nights on Mount Sinai where he received the law—the Ten Commandments—from God. During that time, he was almost constantly in the manifested presence of God. As a result, when he came down from the mountain his face had to be covered; the children of Israel were afraid to come near him because the light of the glory of God shown from his face (Exodus 34:29-30). The Greek words translated as "open face" (prosopon) in our text verse means "unveiled face," and the word translated as "beholding" (katoptrizomai) means "to reflect." This passage could therefore read: "But we all with unveiled faces reflect, as a mirror does, the glory of the Lord as we are changed into His image from glory to glory by His Spirit." The New International Version more clearly reads, "And we, who with unveiled faces all reflect the

Lord's glory, are being transformed into his likeness with ever-increasing glory, which comes from the Lord, who is the Spirit."

If the face of Moses, who spent 40 days in the presence of God on a mountain, reflected God's glory, the face of a Christian who is indwelt by the Spirit of Christ and who is being transformed into Christ's image by that same Spirit, should reflect a good measure of God's glory. Romans 8:28-29 says that God's purpose for us is to be conformed to the image of His Son, and that all things work to our good according to His purpose. And Romans 12:2 says that we are "transformed by the renewing of your mind, that ye may prove what is that good, and acceptable, and perfect, will of God." God's will and purpose is for us to be transformed to the image of His Son, so that He might be the firstborn among many brethren.

As we are being transformed to the likeness of Christ by the renewing of our minds, the character of His Spirit will be manifested in our lives. The result will be that the fruit of the Spirit will be produced in our nature, and this will be reflected in our outward appearance and attitude. The fruit of the Spirit are listed in Galatians 5:22: love, joy, peace, long-suffering (patience), gentleness, goodness, faith, meekness (humility), and temperance (self-control).

Look to Jesus Christ, our Savior. Be transformed by the renewing of your mind, and put a smile on your face that reflects your inward joy and the life of Christ in you. Don't murmur and complain, but know that all the things we are called upon to face work to our good and are part of God's purpose as He transforms us into the glory of Christ's likeness.

Chastened to be Changed

In Hebrews 12:10, it says that God chastens us that we might be partakers of His divine nature; that divine nature that is like Christ and that changes us into His image. One aspect of that nature is humility. We carry so much Adamic pride into our Christianity that God has to work in that area of our lives almost more than anywhere else. Pride goes before destruction says the book of Proverbs, and "A man's pride will bring him low, But the humble in spirit will retain honor" (Proverbs 16:18 and 29:23). Add to those the fact that God is against the proud but He gives grace to the humble according to James 4:6. Since all that is so, we should seek those things that would rid us of our pride and make us humble.

To humble us, God sometimes puts us into situations and circumstances that are designed to keep us humble. For example, God gave the apostle Paul a thorn in his flesh for just that purpose. Paul had been taken to the third heaven, and the glory of the vision was of such a nature that it could easily have made Paul proud of it and of himself. To keep him from that danger, which gives us a pretty good idea of what God thinks of pride, God gave him the thorn and Christ refused to take it away (2 Corinthians 12:1-10).

Paul's training in humility—which is an example of our training—consisted of two parts: the outward humiliation of the thorn, and the inward necessity of humbling himself in absolute dependence upon Christ to overcome the weakness caused by the thorn. God is training us to be totally dependent upon Him, there will be no independent Christians in heaven. So the Lord told Paul, "My grace is sufficient for thee: for my strength is made perfect in weakness" (2 Corinthians 12:9).

In the kingdom of God, we are often given more trials to endure as our revelation and knowledge increase. Most people in the Church would like to become spiritual giants, but most of us are not willing to pay the price to become one. The ones who have done so are the ones who have prayed, obeyed, and studied the Word of God diligently. They are also the ones who have patiently endured trials, so patience could complete its work.

Trials come to us for different reasons. If someone is not in God's will, he or she is not receiving trials so that they will remain humble. In all likelihood, they face certain situations because of their self-made decisions and bad choices. If we stay humble, God will not have to let us endure nearly as much to keep us that way. Matthew 18:4 says:

> Whosoever therefore shall humble himself as this little child, the same is greatest in the kingdom of heaven.

This is a great revelation that Jesus is sharing with us—to be great in the kingdom of heaven, we must be humble. Man looks at outward appear-ances, but God looks on a person's heart (1 Samuel 16:7). Most of those who seem to be great in the eyes of people are not nearly as great in the eyes of God as some who are humble. If you want to be great in the kingdom, you must first be humble. Again, God exalts the humble.

> Humble yourselves in the sight of the Lord, and he shall lift you up.
>
> (James 4:10)

This same thing was said by the Lord:

> For whosoever exalteth himself shall be abased; and he that humbleth himself shall be exalted.
>
> (Luke 14:11)

God lets us endure abasing trials if we start thinking of ourselves as being greater than we actually are—but if we will become humble, God will exalt us. When He says He will exalt us, He is referring to exaltation within the kingdom, not necessarily in the world. Jesus said, "Whosoever therefore shall humble himself as this little child, the same is greatest in the kingdom of heaven" (Matthew 18:4).

NOW THAT I'M SAVED...

Humility toward God is also the key to making the devil flee from us because humility is essentially submission, and James said:

> Submit yourselves therefore to God. Resist the devil, and he will flee from you.
>
> (James 4:7)

To resist the devil and make him flee from us, we must first submit ourselves to God. It is, therefore, impossible for a Christian with a proud heart to resist the devil. Only those with humble hearts will submit to God. Remember, when we go through trials, they are always for a purpose—they keep us humble, chasten us, and give us an opportunity to glorify God, in heaven and earth.

Because of holdovers from our old Adamic nature, we must keep pressing forward to submit ourselves to God and become truly humble—and stay that way. Far too often we want everything God has for us but want to remain independent of Him. It doesn't work that way. God will humble us into submission and dependence. Better for us to press forward and humble ourselves voluntarily. One of the best ways to do that is through a devoted prayer life. Staying on our knees in good times and bad times will build a submissive, dependent attitude within us that will keep us in God's grace and maximize our ability to resist the devil

One of God's designed ways by which we can humble ourselves is by fasting. In Psalm 109:24, David said, "My knees are weak through fasting: and my flesh faileth of fatness."

As our flesh grows weak during a fast, we become more aware of how spiritually helpless we are and how much we need God. So maintaining a continual state of prayer and fasting keeps us in a condition of submission and humility. Far better to have our flesh become weak through fasting than to receive the chastising of the Lord. Psalm 69:10 says that fasting will chasten the soul, and Psalm 35:13 says that fasting will humble the soul. In fasting, there is a spiritual cleansing and growth that comes no other way. God works best in a humble heart.

When our souls are humble, it isn't hard to bend our knees—at the same time, our wills bend to seek God all the more. Our faith is increased by dependence on God. It is because we become more dependent on God when we are in a state of weakness that we are truly strong when we are weak. That's what Paul meant in 2 Corinthians 12:9-10 when he said,

> And he [the Lord] said unto me, My grace is sufficient for thee: for my strength is made perfect in weakness . . . . Therefore I take pleasure in infirmities, in reproaches, in necessities, in persecutions, in distresses for Christ's sake: for when I am weak, then am I strong.

The Greek word *dunamis* that is translated as "strength" here is the same word that is translated as "power" in Luke 24:49, where Jesus told the apostles to wait in Jerusalem until they were endued with power from on high. The strength of our souls is determined by our faith in God, and our faith is increased by our submissive dependence upon God and Christ. Of God strengthening our souls through prayer and submission to Him, David wrote,

> In the day when I cried thou answeredst me, and strengthenedst me with strength in my soul.
>
> (Psalm 138:3)

God strengthens our souls when we humble ourselves and confess with our prayers and tears that without Him we can do nothing (John 15:5). It is only then that the power of God can work through us. All this and much more changes us from faith to faith and glory to glory into the image of Jesus Christ our Lord who said, "The Son can do nothing of himself, but what he seeth the Father do" (John 5:19).

8

How to be Content and Rid of Fear

Being Content

When I was first saved, I remember reading Philippians 4:11 and thinking, "If I could find a way to be content like Paul in whatever situation I find myself, that would be true happiness." I knew there was no way this could be attained outside of God's kingdom. I knew what I wanted, but I did not know how to attain it. The answer had to be in God's Word.

> Not that I speak in respect of want: for I have learned, in whatever state I am, therewith to be content.
>
> (Philippians 4:11)

Paul learned how to be content in every situation of life, and he tells us how this is possible, as does James: ". . . the trying of your faith worketh patience. But let patience have her perfect work, that ye may be perfect and entire, wanting nothing" (James 1:3-4).

Paul attained this level of contentment in which he wanted nothing and was content wherever he was and whatever was happening to him. The word translated in the King James Version as "perfect" (*teleios*) means "complete." Paul was content because he learned how to let patience *complete* its work in his life. The same will be true for us when we learn as Paul did. His trials taught him patience, and our trials can teach us patience. Paul-like experiences can result in a Paul-like life.

Paul wrote, "tribulation worketh patience" (Romans 5:3). Without tribulation we will never learn patience, and without patience we will never learn to be content in all things. That's why Paul said about himself, "I am exceeding joyful in all our tribulation" (2 Corinthians 7:4), and James wrote, "Count it all joy when ye fall into divers temptations [trials]" (James 1:2).

Our carnal nature resists being patient. In our trials, we are always tempted to start murmuring and complaining. So, for us to let patience complete its work, we must bring our human nature (our flesh) into submission to the Word and Spirit of God.

> And not only so, but we glory in tribulations also: knowing that tribulation worketh patience; And patience, experience; and experience, hope:
>
> (Romans 5:3-4)

It is through patience and the comfort of God's Word that we find hope (Romans 15:4). Each time we go patiently through a trial trusting in the Word of God and following the leading of the Holy Spirit, we gain experience. The more experience we have that we can look back on and remember the faithfulness of God, the greater faith we will have that God will take us through our present trial. The more faith we have, the more we are assured that we will obtain what we hope for. Hebrews 11:1 says:

> Now faith is being sure of what we hope for and certain of what we do not see. (NIV)

Strong faith develops by a spiritual process. To have faith, we must first hear the Word of God (Romans 10:17). Then our faith grows as we patiently endure our trials and gain experience. The more experience we have of patiently enduring our trials and seeing the faithfulness of God, the more our faith grows—until it becomes the strong faith we want it to be.

We can complain and worry about our problems, which will only make our situation worse, or we can patiently endure and learn to be content. It's a spiritual principle that we can never learn to be content until we learn to be patient, and we can never learn to be patient without going through trials.

Spiritual Heart Failure Caused by Fear

> Men's hearts failing them for fear, and for looking after those things which are coming on the earth: for the powers of heaven shall be shaken.
>
> (Luke 21:26)

The New International Version translates Luke 21:26 as, "Men will faint from terror, apprehensive of what is coming on the world, for the heavenly bodies will be shaken." There would seem to be a difference in these two translations unless one understands that when the early translators used the words "hearts failing," they were speaking of spiritual hearts. This verse speaks of people losing their faith as a result of looking at the things that would be coming on the earth. Understanding this, both translations obviously render the same meaning.

The King James Version translates the Greek word *apopsucho* as "hearts failing." This Greek word does not relate to the physical heart in any way. It means "to breathe out, such as to faint." When the early translators translated it as "hearts failing" it was in relation to the terminology used in the Old Testament when speaking of someone losing their faith.

Prior to his encounter with Goliath, David used the words for "heart failure" as meaning a loss of faith when he said, "Let no man's heart fail because of him [Goliath]; thy servant will go and fight with this Philistine" (1 Samuel 17:32). Everyone's hearts had failed them, except David's. He was looking to his God, not at the size of Goliath. In these last days, we must look to our God, not at the things that are and will be coming upon the world. If we don't, our hearts will fail us in the same way that King Saul's army experienced heart failure when they looked at the size of their problem.

When trouble comes, we must look to our God in the same way David did. If we don't, we will start to worry, and doubt will take root in our hearts. Doubt is as deadly to our spiritual hearts as an arrow would be to our heart and flesh. We cannot have both doubt and faith in our heart at the same time; we either believe or we don't.

Jesus emphasized the danger of letting our hearts become overcharged (burdened to excess) by the cares of this world (Luke 21:34). In this verse, the Greek word *kardia* is used for "hearts." This word for "heart" is used 160 times in the New Testament. Every time it is used it is in reference to our spiritual hearts as opposed to the muscle that pumps blood through our bodies.

When we look at the difficult situations confronting us, our hearts will fail us like the hearts of Joseph's brothers failed them when they found the money in their sacks (Genesis 42:28). This meant that they were overcome with fear and they lost faith because of the situation that was facing them.

In Luke 21, Jesus warns us about looking at the things that will be coming upon this earth. If we look upon them, we will sink like Peter did when he took his eyes off Jesus and looked at the waves (Matthew 14:30). The only way we can keep our hearts from failing us when we are faced with a crisis is to look to our God and trust Him, no matter how bad things look.

Getting Rid of Fear

In 1 John 4:18, it is written:

> There is no fear in love; but perfect love casteth out fear: because fear hath torment. He that feareth is not made perfect in love.

To have perfect love and be free of fear, we must learn to trust God. In a mature love relationship with God, trust is absolutely essential. In fact, it's impossible to have a mature and true love relationship with another, whether human or divine, without trust. That's why it's so important to learn patience and gain relationship experiences. Trust is something that is learned by another being faithful to you.

When we learn to trust God, fear will leave us because we'll be able to walk in perfect love with Him. Without patience, however, we'll never gain the experiences that will teach us to trust God. And without that trust, we'll never have a perfect or "mature" love relationship with our Father, the kind of relationship that will free us from fear.

How hard we press to learn patience depends on how close we want to get to God. James tells us, "Draw nigh to God, and he will draw nigh to you" (James 4:8). If we walk in obedience to God, trusting Him, and giving Him praise in whatever state we find ourselves, He will draw close to us.

Remember, without trust, we cannot have great faith, nor can we have a mature love relationship with our God. And it all starts with the trying of our faith that works patience.

Pray often. Keep the faith. Let patience complete its work in your life. Don't be overburdened by the cares of this world. Know that God works all things to our good as we are being transformed to the image of His Son (Romans 8:28-29). Therefore, we can have joy, even in the midst of our trials.

Peter's Lesson in Faith and Fear

> Thou shalt be called Cephas, which is by interpretation, A stone.
>
> (John 1:42)

Throughout the Scriptures, name changes denote a change in relationship to God (e.g.,

Jacob to Israel) or a change in the character of the person. Jesus surnamed James the son of Zebedee, and John the brother of James, "Boanerges," which means "The sons of thunder" (Mark 3:17). Obviously, this name referred to their characters. They must have been highly enthusiastic or excitable men—or highly volatile.

One of the most important name changes in the Gospels was made when Jesus saw Simon, the brother of James—He said to him,

> Thou art Simon the Son of Jona: thou shalt
> be called Cephas, which is by interpretation,
> a stone.
>
> (John 1:42)

Jesus was speaking of the character of Simon when He called him the "son of Jona [or Jonah]." When Jesus saw Peter coming with his brother, Andrew, He already knew about him, just as He knew about Nathaniel's character when He first saw him: "Behold, an Israelite indeed, in whom is no guile" (John 1:47).

John 1:42 may be a factual statement about Simon Peter's physical lineage, but it's also a statement about his spiritual character, both what it was, and what it would one day become. When we compare the behavior of Jonah (in the Old Testament) to the way Peter acted (in the New Testament), we see that these two men are much alike.

Both tried to run from God's will. Jonah would rather have seen the people of Nineveh die than be converted. Peter would rather have cut off the ears of those who came to take Jesus away than to let the will of God be done (John 18:10).

Just as Jonah was brought to repentance after spending three days in the belly of the whale, Peter was grieved after Jesus asked him a third time if he loved Him (John 21:15-17).

Jonah could not understand why he should try to lead the people of Nineveh to repentance until God gave him an illustration involving a gourd. Peter never understood why he should put forth any effort to help the Gentiles until God showed him the vision of the unclean animals (Acts 10:11-35).

There are numerous similarities between Jonah and Peter. Almost every time Peter speaks, we can see the spirit of Jonah influencing him. The same spirit that had driven Jonah, controlled Peter as well. When I use the word "spirit" in this sense, I am not referring to a supernatural entity, but to the make-up of an individual, stemming from his carnal nature, that causes him to behave in characteristic ways. This carnal nature—a spirit of ambition, impetuousness, and pride, if you will—causes many to be unfruitful. It causes one who is trying to follow Jesus to not deny self and take up his or her cross. It is from the carnal nature and it must be crucified along with all the affections and lusts (Galatians 5:24).

That's why Peter reminds us of ourselves— we all have to deal with this same spirit—or carnal attitude. This spirit or attitude is known as the carnal man, the natural man, or the sinful nature. It's that part of us that doesn't understand or want to do the things of God—or if it's grudgingly willing to do them, it doesn't want to do them in God's way.

When Jesus first met Simon, He called him "the son of Jonah." He also said that he would be called Cephas, "the rock." Cephas comes from the Greek word *kephas*. That time had not yet come, however. It was not until after many trials and failures brought about by fear and lack of faith that Peter became truly Cephas, the rock. Until then, he would simply be a piece of the true Rock.

Peter, a Piece of the Rock

In Matthew 16:13-19, it's recorded that Jesus gave Simon the new name of "Peter." Jesus had asked the disciples who they thought He was. Simon answered, "Thou art the Christ, the Son of the living God" (Matthew 16:16).

In response, Jesus said, "Blessed art thou, Simon Bar-jona [which means "son of Jonah"]: for flesh and blood hath not revealed it unto thee, but my Father which is in heaven" (Matthew 16:17).

Although it was revealed to Peter that Jesus was the Christ, the Son of the living God, and he believed it, he was still not ready to take up his cross and follow Jesus in the self-denying way that discipleship demands. In that state, he was like a piece of detached rock. If you follow Jesus, you must deny yourself or you will be like Peter was at this time—"a detached piece of rock."

"Peter" comes from the Greek word *petros*. *Petros* not only means "a piece of rock," it also means "a detached piece of rock" (*Vine's Expository Dictionary*). When Jesus said, "Thou art Peter," He was telling Simon that he was a detached piece of rock. Simon was not yet *cephas*, but he was only *petros*.

When Jesus said, "Upon this rock I will build my church," He used the word *petra*. This is the word that is used in the story of the foolish man who built his house upon the sand in contrast to the one who built his house upon a rock (*petra*). The rock from which Peter was detached at this time was also *petra*. The foundation upon which Jesus is building His Church is *petra*, not *kephas*. The rock which the Church is built upon is the truth that Jesus is the Christ, the Son of God (John 20:31).

Having this knowledge as Peter did, however, is not enough. James 2:20 tells us, "faith without works is dead." The works that are needed in order for us to put life in our faith include self-denial and obedience. If we believe that Jesus is the Christ, the Son of the living God, and we don't deny self and take up our cross to follow Him, we are like detached pieces of rock. That's why in John 20:31, John writes, " . . . that you might believe . . . and believing you might have life throughhis name." In other words, you must not only "believe that Jesus is the Christ, the Son of God, you must act upon what you believe in order to "have life through his name."

The spiritual attitude of Jonah (the carnal nature) keeps people from abiding in Jesus and His Word. It also keeps those who are saved from doing the things it takes to be called great in the kingdom of God. It makes them fearful that doing things God's way won't succeed, or that if they don't do it themselves God won't do it.

Because of that spiritual attitude, Simon Peter failed several times, but it's evident that he eventually shed his carnal nature and went on to become a rock in the faith. He was no longer detached from *petra*, and he became a *cephas* in the faith. As Peter did, so can we!

9

Comparing Spiritual to Spiritual

> Which things also we speak, not in the words which man's wisdom teacheth, but which the Holy Ghost teacheth; comparing spiritual things with spiritual.
>
> (1 Corinthians 2:13)

The natural part of a person cannot understand the things of God because they are foolishness to him (1 Corinthians 2:14). The reason they are foolishness is that the natural, unsaved person has not received the spiritual eyes with which to see the things of God. God must give insight through the Holy Spirit before the Word of God and God's ways make sense to a person. The human mind is not capable of understanding the things of God unless God gives the understanding—and He only gives that to those who believe in His Son Jesus Christ and receive eternal life through Him.

The people who heard Jesus tell parables could not understand them many times for the same reason people don't understand much of what He tells us by His Spirit today. We have been trained to think only in relation to physical things. If our mind and our five physical senses are not involved, understanding of spiritual matters seems impossible, even foolish, to the natural man. To be able to understand the spiritual truths of God's Word, we must put off the old man's way of thinking by renewing our minds with the Word of God. "And be not conformed to this world: but be ye transformed by the renewing of your mind, that ye may prove what is that good, and acceptable, and perfect, will of God" (Romans 12:2). As we do that more and more, we will receive more and more help from the Holy Spirit, who will lead us into all truth. "Howbeit when he, the Spirit of truth, is come, he will guide you into all truth: for he shall not speak of himself; but whatsoever he shall hear, that shall he speak: and he will shew you things to come" (John 16:13).

Spiritually Discerning the Things of the Spirit

Now we have received, not the spirit of the world, but the spirit which is of God; that we might know the things that are freely given to us of God. Which things also we speak, not in words which man's wisdom teacheth, but which the Holy Ghost teacheth; comparing spiritual things with spiritual.

But the natural man receiveth not the things of the Spirit of God: for they are foolishness unto him: neither can he know them, because they are spiritually discerned. But he that is spiritual judgeth all things, yet he himself is judged of no man. For who hath known the mind of the Lord, that he may instruct him? But we have the mind of Christ. (1 Corinthians 2:12-16)

The Greek word translated "discerned" (*anakrino*) in 1 Corinthians 2:14 is the same word that is translated "judgeth" and also "judged" in verse 15. To better understand what the author is saying in verse 15, the Greek word *anakrino* should be translated the same as in verse 14, since verse 15 is expounding what was said in verse 14. So if we apply that translation to verse 15, we have the following interpretation: "But he that is spiritual [able to understand spiritual things] discerns all things, yet he himself is discerned of no man."

When Jesus taught, He compared spiritual things to physical things so that His disciples would better understand what He wanted them to learn. We must do the same thing with the help of the Holy Spirit if we are to discern the spiritual lessons that are in the Word for us. For example, let's look at the following Scripture:

"The light of the body is the eye: therefore when thine eye is single, thy whole body also is full of light; but when thine eye is evil, thy body also is full of darkness."

(Luke 11:34)

There are two different Greek words that are translated as "light" in this verse. The first one means "illuminator," the second one means "well-illuminating." The word translated as "single" means "clear." So this verse could be paralleled as follows, "The illuminator of the body is the eye: therefore, when the eye is clear and brings in a lot of light, the whole body is well-illuminated: but when the eye is evil [clouded or blind], the body is full of darkness."

We can see the spiritual lesson in this physical truth if we put it this way: The mind is the eye of the spiritual body because it is with our understanding that we are able to see and learn spiritual truths (Ephesians 1:18).

When we apply this to Luke 11:34 (quoted above), we get the following spiritual truth: The illuminator of the spirit is the mind; therefore, if the mind is clear, the whole spirit is well-illuminated: but when the mind is evil, the spirit is full of darkness.

Two Bodies

There are two bodies—one of the flesh, the other of the spirit. If we understand that Jesus was using an illustration of the body of flesh to teach a truth about the body of the spirit, we can understand the spiritual meaning behind what He said. Jesus often taught in this way. He used examples of things we can see and understand in order to teach about things we cannot see with physical eyes, so we can see by spiritual understanding. When we see the truth of the gospel in our mind by understanding, and we respond by believing, faith is in operation.

When we study God's Word, we must continually strive to compare the physical truths found in His Word to spiritual truths. God's Word is spiritual, and it must be spiritually discerned.

Another good example of comparing spiritual things to spiritual is found in Acts 17:11. Here the writer of Acts speaks of the people at Berea receiving the Word (which is spiritual) with all readiness of mind and searching the Scriptures (which are spiritual) daily to see if those things they heard were so. They were comparing what they heard to the Scriptures. We know what they heard was the testimony of Jesus Christ. The word translated as "searched" in Acts 17:11 is the same word that is translated as "discerned" in 1 Corinthians 2:14. What they were doing was discerning God's Word (in the Old Testament) and comparing it to what they had heard.

Three Who Bear Witness

There are three in heaven who bear witness that Jesus is the Christ and the Son of God (the Father, the Word, and the Holy Ghost). Jesus said in John 5:31:

> If I bear witness of myself, my witness is not true.

The Law said that the testimony of two or three was true (John 8:17). According to the Law, there had to be at least two witnesses for something to be accepted as true. Jesus came to fulfill the Law to the fullest extent. This is why there had to be more than one witness.

In John 8:18, Jesus said that the Father bears witness of Him. We can find this witness in the Scriptures of the Old Testament as well (John 5:31-39). If we don't believe the Father's witness, we will not believe the witness of the Son. Also, unless we obey the teachings of Jesus, we can never have the witness of the Holy Spirit who also bears witness of the Son (John 15:26, Acts 5:32, and 1 John 5:8).

Jesus, the Spiritual Word

> And the Word was made flesh, and dwelt among us, (and we beheld his glory, the glory as of the only begotten of the Father), full of grace and truth.
>
> (John 1:14)

We must build our faith upon the Word of God. We cannot separate the Word from Jesus, because He is the Word. The keys to the kingdom are found in the Word of God. John preached, "Repent ye: for the kingdom of heaven is at hand" (Matthew 3:2). This is the same message that Jesus preached in

Matthew 4:17 and Mark 1:14-15. Our message to the world today is the same one the apostles preached—"Jesus Christ, and him crucified" (1 Corinthians 2:2). Jesus said there had not been a greater prophet than John the Baptist, yet John the Baptist never performed a miracle. He was great because of the message he preached.

When Jesus told His disciples that they would do greater works than the miracles they saw Him do, He was speaking of the message they would preach to lead people into the kingdom of God (John 14:12). The knowledge that Jesus Christ is the Son of God and that He died for our sins gives us the keys which open the way into the kingdom of God. Someone must first realize that they need a Savior before they know to repent. In the same way that it was John's message that made him great, it is the message that Jesus died for our sins and rose again which makes us do greater works than the miracles they saw Jesus perform. This is also why the least in the kingdom is greater than John the Baptist; the least has the keys to the kingdom of God.

To lead someone to the knowledge of Jesus, thereby enabling God to save him or her, is the greatest work we can do on earth. We will truly understand this if we remember why Jesus shed His blood. The greatest work ever recorded is that which was done by Jesus when He sacrificed His life so we could be saved. The greatest work we can do is to lead someone to

Him. This is why Jesus came into the world—to reconcile the world to God—and this is the ministry He gave His Church as well (2 Corinthians 5:18). It took the shedding of His blood for us to have the privilege of ministering this service to others in His behalf. What an honor it is to be able to lead a lost soul to the knowledge of Jesus Christ. We could split 1,000 seas by His power, and it would not cost one drop of His blood. What other work could we do that cost such a high price?

In Matthew 5:19, Jesus said:

> Whosoever therefore shall break one of these least commandments, and shall teach men so, he shall be called the least in the kingdom of heaven: but whosoever shall do and teach them, the same shall be called great in the kingdom of heaven.

This is totally different from the perception most people have of the qualifications one must have in order to be called great in the kingdom of heaven. Many whom the world sees as great are actually small because of the truth spoken in Matthew 5:19. A great man or woman (one who will not compromise with the world), will not be popular even among church attendees.

Some of the things it takes to be called great in the kingdom include living by Matthew 5:19, and being a servant (Matthew 20:27). A servant must flee youthful lusts, and follow righteousness, faith, love, and peace with those who call on the Lord out of a pure heart (2 Timothy 2:21-26). Those who call on God out of a pure heart are our brothers and sisters in the Lord, no matter what the name above the door where they worship.

Teachings can rob someone of greatness if they teach people to think less of brothers and sisters of other Christian beliefs and backgrounds, thereby not following righteousness, faith, love, and peace with those who call on the Lord. We must avoid foolish and unlearned questions that can cause strife. To be great in the kingdom of God, therefore, we must not let a few differences in our thinking cause divisions among us and others who call on the Lord out of a pure heart:

> And the servant of the Lord must not strive; but be gentle unto all men, apt to teach, patient, In meekness instructing those that oppose themselves; if God peradventure will give them repentance to the acknowledging of the truth; And that they may recover themselves out of the snare of the devil, who are taken captive by him at his will.
>
> (2 Timothy 2:24-26)

10

The River of Life That Flows Through Christ

> And he showed me a pure river of water of life, clear as crystal, proceeding out of the throne of God and of the Lamb.
>
> (Revelation 22:1)

There is a river of living water flowing through the kingdom of God here on earth. This is the same living water that Jesus offered to the woman at the well:

> If thou knewest the gift of God, and who it is that saith to thee, Give me to drink; thou wouldest have asked of him, and he would have given thee living water.
>
> (John 4:10)

Jesus continued His explanation:

> But whosoever drinketh of the water that I shall give him shall never thirst; but the water that I shall give him shall be in him a well of water springing up into everlasting life.
>
> (John 4:14)

NOW THAT I'M SAVED. . .

This living water is flowing through the Holy City of God (the Church). It is pure and it is as clear as crystal; it comes from the throne of God and the throne of the Lamb. Because our hearts are the throne of God in the kingdom of God on earth, the living water flows from our hearts. Jesus clearly tells us that the kingdom of God is within us:

> He that believeth on me, as the scripture hath said, out of his belly shall flow rivers of living water.
>
> (John 7:38)

This holy water is for anyone who will come and drink of it:

> Ho, every one that thirsteth, come ye to the waters, and he that hath no money; come ye, buy, and eat; yea, come, buy wine and milk without money and without price.
>
> (Isaiah 55:1)

This water is free, and no price can be put on it, because it took something priceless to cover its cost, thereby enabling us to be made worthy to drink of it. The price was paid by the blood of Jesus. Many people try to drink of the water of life and walk down the street of the New Jerusalem without first going to the tree of life, but they cannot do this because the tree is on either side of the river of life, and it is in the midst of the street of the Holy City. Before someone can drink of this living water, or walk down the street of the Holy City, one must first come to the Cross of Jesus Christ.

When the Cross is called a tree in the New Testament, the Greek word from which it is translated is *xulon*. It means "a piece of wood" or anything made of wood, such as a stick, club, a non-living tree, or other wood products. When a live, green tree is referred to in the New Testament, the word *dendron*, is used in the original Greek. In the Book of Revelation, the word that is used to describe the tree of life,  which is in the kingdom of God, is the word *xulon*, which means a piece of wood or anything that is made of wood (Acts 5:30; 10:39; 13:29; Galatians 3:13; 1 Peter 2:24).

Because of sin, we lost our right to the first tree of life. Now, because of the obedience of Christ, we have access to another. This second tree of life is the one on which Jesus died. The Cross is the tree of life that is in the midst of the kingdom of God on this planet. This second tree is far better than the first one. The first tree gave life to the body of flesh. The second tree, a spiritual one, gives life to the spirit. The second one is also better than the first because it produces a better fruit. We are the fruit of the second tree, and just as life was in the fruit of the first tree, life is also in us. This life which is in us is the Light of the world, the Bread of Life, the living water, the Word of God.

The law of creation causes a tree to bear fruit after its own kind. In this same manner, the tree of life bears fruit after its own kind, and the fruit it bears conforms to the fruit of the twelve Apostles. This tree bears its fruit continually, not only in one season of the year.

The Leaves of Healing

> In the midst of the street of it, and on either side of the river, was there the tree of life, which bare twelve manner of fruits, and yielded her fruit every month: and the leaves were for the healing of the nations.
>
> (Revelation 22:2)

The Greek word translated as "leaves" in this verse is *phullon*. It means "a sprout," such as a leaf, and it is very closely related to the word *phule*, which means an "offshoot," such as a race or clan, kindred or tribe. The leaves or "sprouts" of this spiritual tree are the followers of Christ, the redeemed ones, and it is through them that healing will come to the nations.

The nations can be healed only when they are grafted into, and become part of, the Body of Christ as it is described in Romans 11. The only way this can happen is for the nations to hear the gospel and see their need to be saved. When this happens, and an individual surrenders his or her heart to Jesus Christ, the tree of life is producing fruit after the manner of the twelve apostles. We are the kindred of the Lord Jesus Christ, offshoots of that spiritual tree of life which Christ died upon (Romans 8:29, Colossians 1:18, Hebrews 2:9-11, and Revelation 1:5).

> Go unto this people, and say, Hearing ye shall hear, and shall not understand; and seeing ye shall see, and not perceive: For the heart of this people is waxed gross, and their ears are dull of hearing, and their eyes have closed; lest they should see with their eyes, and hear with their ears, and understand with their heart, and should be converted, and I should heal them.
>
> (Acts 28: 26-27)

We cannot heal the people of the nations of the world, but we can lead them to the Healer, who is Jesus Christ.

How can they be healed unless they be converted? How can they be converted unless they understand? How can they understand unless they hear? And how can they hear unless someone is sent? This is what the leaves (offshoots) are for. Jesus said:

> Go ye into all the world, and preach the gospel to every creature. He that believeth and is baptized shall be saved.
>
> (Mark 16:15-16)

NOW THAT I'M SAVED. . .

In this holy city there is no longer a curse because when the throne of our heart is surrendered to God, and He rules, there is no more curse, but life, righteousness, and peace.

> Christ hath redeemed us from the curse of the law, being made a curse for us: for it is written, Cursed is every one that hangeth on a tree: That the blessing of Abraham might come on the Gentiles through Jesus Christ; that we might receive the promise of the Spirit through faith.
>
> (Galatians 3:13-14)

Yes, there is a city in heaven with golden streets, but it was built to be a pattern of the city that God is building here on earth. The angel said, "Come hither, I will shew thee the bride, the Lamb's wife" (Revelation 21:9). He then described the city with golden streets, the tree of life, and the river of the water of life. The city that came down from heaven is the one which is the most important to God. His Son gave His life so that God's kingdom might come to earth and be filled by all who believe. The city in heaven was built as a blueprint of the one described in Revelation 21.

Two Cities

> And I saw a new heaven and a new earth: for the first heaven and the first earth were passed away.
>
> (Revelation 21:1)

When I wrote about the Cross being the tree of life in the midst of the kingdom of God on earth, I realized there are two cities. One is in heaven, the other is the one Jesus gave His life to build. This is the city that was seen by John in Revelation 21. In verse 9, the angel tells John that he is going to show him the Bride, the Lamb's wife. He then goes on to describe the city. The angel is describing the Church of Jesus Christ here.

The Bible tells us that the things we can't see (spiritual things) may be understood by things we can see, even His eternal power and Godhead, so that we are without excuse (Romans 1:20). I believe the purpose of this world is also displayed in heaven. The city with golden streets in heaven is a pattern of the city which God is building for Himself to inhabit—a pattern of His temple and eternal dwelling place.

This city was there before time began, and it will be there when time is no more. Satan, who thought himself to be so wise, had God's plan right before his eyes, but he was blind to what it said. If this is true, and I believe it is, then Romans 1:20-21 is true for Satan and for the fallen angels also, and they too, are without excuse.

Read the description of the Holy City in Revelation 21, and understand that it is a description of the Bride (the Church). If you believe the report of the saints, who have had a glimpse of a city in heaven like the one John described as being the Church, then it should not be difficult to believe it is a pattern of the kingdom of God here on earth. If there is, then surely it has been there since the beginning, before the fall of Satan.

What a mighty God we serve! Could it be that He has a pattern of His flawless plan placed in the midst of heaven, positioned there like a showcase since before creation? I believe it is there; it is not the one God plans to inhabit forever. It is the Church, the Bride of Christ, that is the Temple of God. We will inhabit the city in heaven and God will inhabit us, "the temple of God."

Who can comprehend the wisdom of God? Nothing is hidden from His eyes. He is from everlasting to everlasting, and He fills everything in between. Only eternity itself can contain Him. He is so worthy to be praised!

The Bread of Life

> I am the living bread which came down from heaven: if any man eat of this bread, he shall live for ever: and the bread that I will give is my flesh, which I will give for the life of the world.
>
> (John 6:51)

Jesus is the living bread:

> Whoso eateth my flesh, and drinketh my blood, hath eternal life; and I will raise him up in the last day.
>
> (John 6:54)

Jesus is the Word of God:

> And the Word was made flesh, and dwelt
> among us.
>
> (John 1:14)

When Jesus was talking about eating His flesh, He was talking about the Word of God.

Both Matthew 4:4 and Deuteronomy 8:3 say that manna was given to teach us that we don't live by bread alone, but by every word that proceeds out of the mouth of God.

Manna was food for the body. John 6:49 tells us that the ones who ate manna in the wilderness are now dead.

The living bread, on the other hand, is food for the soul. John 6:54-58 tells us that if you eat of the flesh of Jesus (God's Word) you will live forever.

Exodus 16:21 tells us that the manna had to be gathered daily. The supply gathered the day before was not good for the next day. They gathered it in the morning and fed on it until the next morning. It was a task that had to be done daily.

Jesus said we were to ask for our bread daily as well. In His model prayer, He said we should pray, "Give us this day our daily bread" (Matthew 6:11). He did not say we were to ask for a supply to last two or three days; He said, "Give us this day our daily bread." Our souls need to be fed daily in the same way that our bodies need food daily. Therefore, we need to pray that God will give us understanding when we read the Scriptures daily. Only when we understand the Word can our souls digest its meaning. We must not only trust God for our daily physical needs; we must also trust Him for our daily spiritual bread to feed our souls.

We need a fresh supply of bread daily. We must gather it daily and feed on it until the next day when it is time to gather a fresh supply. Read the Word of God daily, and receive your daily bread so you can feed from it as God gives you under-standing. Don't forget to gather an extra supply of the Word on the day before the Sabbath, so you may devote your day of rest to praise and worship.

> O taste and see that the Lord is good.
>
> (Psalm 34:8)

The Road to Emmaus

> And they drew nigh unto the village, whither they went: and he made as though he would have gone further. But they constrained him, saying, Abide with us: for it is toward evening, and the day is far spent. And he went in to tarry with them. And it came to pass, as he sat at meat with them, he took bread, and blessed it, and brake, and gave to them. And their eyes were opened, and they knew him; and he vanished out of their sight. And they said one to another, Did not our heart burn within us, while he talked with us by the way, and while he opened to us the scriptures?
>
> (Luke 24:28-32)

As the two travelers walked on the road to Emmaus that day, they were met by Jesus Christ and He went into their home and broke bread and gave it to them, and their hearts burned within them because of the spiritual bread that Jesus blessed, broke, and fed them. This is the same road that every saved person has walked.

When the pastor or a teacher of a church breaks (discerns) the Word and serves it, and when the Holy Spirit blesses it, our eyes are opened. While He speaks to us by the Holy Spirit, our hearts burn within us: but if we don't invite Him in, He will pass from our presence. It will be only by His grace that He will return.

When the risen Savior speaks to lost souls who are traveling this road, and their eyes are opened, and their hearts burn within them, they must invite Jesus into their hearts or He will not abide with them. Just as Jesus would not enter the home of these two travelers until He was invited, He will not come into our heart unless He is invited.

We know Jesus by the breaking of the spiritual bread that feeds us, and that bread is Jesus.

> And they told what things were done in the way, and how he was known of them in breaking of bread.
>
> (Luke 24:35)

NOW THAT I'M SAVED...

The Blood and the Word

> Verily, verily, I say unto you, Except ye
> eat the flesh of the Son of man, and drink his
> blood, ye have no life in you.
>
> (John 6:53)

The holy blood of Jesus is the component
which makes the Cross the tree of life for any
who will eat of the flesh of Jesus. It is also the
reason why the living water that is in us flows
out of us and springs up into everlasting life
through the word of our testimony. First, we
could not be saved if it weren't for the blood of
Jesus. Second, we could not be saved if it had not
been for someone telling us about the plan of
salvation. This is why our testimony is so
important. Every soul that is saved receives
salvation because of the blood of Jesus and
because of someone's testimony about Jesus
Christ.

Two things are necessary for someone to be
converted: the blood of Jesus and the word of
our testimony about Jesus Christ. Jesus made the
Cross a tree of life by shedding His blood on it.
He also made it the duty of the Church to tell
the world about God's plan of salvation. This is
more than a job; it is a commandment. Jesus also
said that if we did not confess Him before
others, He would not confess us before His
Father.

To testify of Jesus is our calling! Many people
wonder what their ministry and calling is—there

is only one ministry, and it is His. He has given to each of us a calling to fulfill that ministry. Every born-again child of God has the ministry of reconciliation (2 Corinthians 5:18). The only way this will happen is by the ministering of the Word, because we are saved by grace through faith, and faith comes by hearing the Word of God (Romans 10:17).

We must not forget that there is only one Body of Christ, and one ministry. It is the one Jesus gave His life for, and the one He gave to us so that we might carry it on for Him. This ministry is to reconcile a lost and dying world to God. There would not be as much division within the Church of Jesus Christ if everyone realized that we all have the same ministry— "the ministry of reconciliation." Many different callings help to carry out this ministry, but there is only one ministry. In light of this truth, therefore, let us no longer say, "my ministry," but let us say "His ministry."

> And he said unto them, Go ye into all the world, and preach the gospel to every creature. He that believeth and is baptized shall be saved; but he that believeth not shall be damned.
>
> (Mark 16:15-16)

The most important work of the Church is to tell the world that Jesus died for our sins and to let them know about God's plan of redemption. Before Jesus ascended, He gave this ministry to His Church.

NOW THAT I'M SAVED...

> And they overcame him [the devil] by the blood of the Lamb, and by the word of their testimony.
>
> (Revelation 12:11)

Remember, if we confess Jesus to the world, He will confess us to the angels of God and to the Father (Matthew 10:32 and Luke 12:8).

11

The Time in Which We Live

In the summer of 1987, there was a very unusual sign in the heavens. There was a rainbow around the sun. After a short time there was a small piece near the bottom that broke away from the larger part of the rainbow. Dark clouds filled the area inside of the circle, even though the sky was clear and there was not a cloud to be seen any-where. After the small piece of rainbow broke away, the dark clouds started coming out of the opening that the small piece of the rainbow made when it had broken away. They went downward and stopped when they reached the small piece of the rainbow. The clouds continued coming out of the opening, until the rainbow started breaking up. It was very unusual. Though the media reported that it was a common occurrence, I had never seen it happen before, nor have I ever met another person who has seen such a thing happen before. (Seen over Charleston, West Virginia, in the summer of 1987.)

During the time when this phenomenon was taking place I was sleeping since I had worked the night before. When my wife came home, she told me what she had seen. We believed it was a sign. As we discussed what it might mean, we were looking in the Scriptures that related to rainbows and signs in the sky.

As I read Luke 21:25, God spoke to me, "This is the time in which you now live." Luke 21:25-26 says:

> And there shall be signs in the sun, and in the moon, and in the stars; and upon the earth distress of nations, with perplexity; the sea and the waves roaring; Men's hearts failing them for fear, and for looking after those things which are coming on the earth: for the powers of heaven shall be shaken.

I told my wife, along with several other people, what God had told me that day. Since that day, therefore, I have believed we are living in the time of which these verses speak. Although I never fully understood what these verses meant, I knew it had something to do with the darkness of the sun, the moon, and the stars (Matthew 24:29 and Mark 13:24-25). After at least a year and a half had passed, God gave me another word on this same verse. Because Luke 21:25-26 is near verse 27, which I was studying at the time, I was meditating on this verse and those close to it. One day, around 2:00 or 3:00 in the morning, I had awakened and could not go back to sleep. The Lord spoke to me, "As there was darkness throughout the land of Egypt, there is darkness upon the land today." Immediately I knew He was revealing the meaning of Luke 21:25 to me. It was referring to spiritual darkness.

There are few who will hear from heaven.

He had already told me I was living in the time of these events. Now He had revealed their meaning to me. This is why I now believe we are living in the time of spiritual darkness.

In Ezekiel 32:7-8, we find Scripture that gives the illustration of a cloud covering the sun as meaning spiritual darkness is upon the land:

> And when I shall put thee out, I will cover the heavens, and make the stars thereof dark; I will cover the sun with a cloud, and the moon shall not give her light. All the bright lights of heaven will I make dark over thee, and set darkness upon thy land, saith the Lord God.

There is spiritual darkness upon the land, but there is good news also. God also told me that night, "As there was light in the camp of Israel, there is light in My Church."

NOW THAT I'M SAVED. . .

There is no doubt in my mind that Jesus is coming soon, but first there is the spiritual darkness; a darkness that we must not allow to overcome the light of our testimony of Christ and our faith in Him.

Spiritual Darkness

> And when I shall put thee out, I will cover the heaven, and make the stars thereof dark; I will cover the sun with a cloud, and the moon shall not give her light. All the bright lights of heaven will I make dark over thee, and set darkness upon thy land, saith the Lord God.
>
> (Ezekiel 32:7-8)

In the Old Testament darkness is used not only to describe physical darkness, but also to describe the condition of the land when people turn their hearts away from God. The Bible often describes spiritual darkness by speaking of heavenly bodies being darkened. This is the case in our opening epigram from Ezekiel 32.

In a similar vein, Isaiah 9:19 says that the land was darkened through the wrath of God. When a nation or individual turns from God, He withdraws His blessing, and the spiritual lights from heaven are darkened. Another example of this is found in Micah 3:6. It says that because the prophets were corrupt, God said the sun would go down over them and the day would be dark over them. We can see by these Scriptures that God is speaking of spiritual darkness.

Joel 2:1-2 says that when the day of the Lord comes nigh at hand, it will be a day of darkness and of gloominess; a day of clouds and of thick darkness as the morning upon the mountains. The Bible speaks about spiritual darkness when it refers to the darkness of the sun, moon, and stars. Knowing this, we can understand that Joel 2:1-2, and 3:15 are referring to the same thing that Jesus speaks of in Matthew 24:29:

> Immediately after the tribulation of those days shall the sun be darkened, and the moon shall not give her light, and the stars shall fall from heaven.

The Greek word that is translated as "after" can also be translated, "amid," "with," and "together." The word translated as "fall" means "to fail."

As He often did, Jesus was speaking about a spiritual condition. Another example of this is found in Zephaniah 1:14-18, where the Word speaks of the same time in the future that Jesus and Joel referred to:

> The great day of the Lord is near, it is near, and hasteth greatly, even the voice of the day of the Lord: the mighty man shall cry there bitterly. That day is a day of wrath, [as we see in Isaiah 9:19] a day of trouble and distress, a day of wasteness and desolation, a day of darkness and gloominess, a day of clouds [as in Micah 3:6] and thick darkness.
> (Zephaniah 1:14-15)

The same conditions are described by the prophet Amos:

> And it shall come to pass in that day, saith the Lord God, that I will cause the sun to go down at noon, and I will darken the earth in the clear day: And I will turn your feasts into mourning, and all your songs into lamentation; and I will bring up sackcloth upon all loins, and baldness upon every head; and I will make it as the mourning of an only son, and the end thereof as a bitter day. Behold, the days come, saith the Lord God, that I will send a famine in the land, not a famine of bread, nor a thirst for water, but of hearing the words of the Lord.
>
> (Amos 8:9-11)

When spiritual darkness comes upon the land, there are few who will hear from heaven. This is why many people across our land today are starving spiritually. The only way for America to be blessed again is for God's people to repent and turn to Him.

> If my people [not the sinners, but the Church], which are called by my name, shall humble themselves, and pray, and seek my face, and turn from their wicked ways; then will I hear from heaven, and will forgive their sin, and will heal their land.
>
> (2 Chronicles 7:14)

In the same way that a cloud prevents the sunlight from shining upon the earth, sin is a cloud that stops God's light from shining upon His people. We can blame whoever or whatever we want for the condition of our country, but the reason it is not being blessed is because of the cloud of sin that is hovering over a backsliding church. Before we will see revival in our land, the people of God's Church must humble themselves, pray, seek His face, and turn from their wicked ways. We are now living in the time of which Jesus spoke in Luke 21:25-26. There is darkness over the land, and it is causing a great famine—not of bread and water—but of words and blessings from heaven. The cloud of sin is keeping the heavenly lights from reaching a backsliding Church.

These are the same last days of which Paul spoke in 2 Timothy 3:1-7:

> This know also, that in the last days perilous times shall come. For men shall be lovers of their own selves, covetous, boasters, proud, blasphemers, disobedient to parents, unthank-ful, unholy, Without natural affection, truce-breakers, false accusers, incontinent, fierce, despisers of those that are good, Traitors, heady, highminded, lovers of pleasures more than lovers of God; Having a form of godliness, but denying the power thereof: from such turn away. For of this sort are they which creep into houses, and lead captive silly women laden with sins, led away with divers lusts, Ever learning, and never able to come to the knowledge of the truth.

NOW THAT I'M SAVED...

This sounds more like an article written in a local newspaper than something written nearly two thousand years ago. The reason this is true is that it was written about these last days in which we now live. Don't be discouraged, however, because there is so much darkness in the land. But remember, as there was light in the camp of Israel, there is light in God's true Church that hasn't bowed its knees to another god. There are some, as always, who have not turned their hearts away from the living God.

12

The Last Days Are Upon Us

This know also, that in the last days
perilous times shall come.

(2 Timothy 3:1)

For centuries people have been making
statements and guessing what or who the beast
of the End Times would be. Some believe there
will be a revival of the Roman Empire, and some
even say that it will be a revival of the Roman
Catholic Church. The Book of Revelation says
that the beast John saw had seven heads; five
had already fallen, one was, and one had not yet
come. Revelation also says that when this
seventh head came, it would continue for a short
time. God has shown me who the seventh head
was, and who the eighth will be (one of the
original seven).

Since the summer of 1987, when God told me
I was living in the time of the end, I have been
looking for signs of such a power to rise up.

I knew one of the first signs of such power would be a move to control the world money supply. One night, while I was studying, I received a word from God about the beast of the End Times, and who would be one of the original seven. I believe this was from God, and since I first wrote this, much of what God showed me has started to come to pass.

While sitting at my desk about two months before any indication was given that the Berlin Wall was going to come down, I received the following word from God.

The beast of the End Times that is spoken of in Revelation has seven heads (Revelation 13:1-10). Germany of World War I and II was the seventh head which was to come and continue a short time. Its head was wounded with the sword as unto death during World War I, and was healed and tried to destroy everything that stood for the living God in World War II. (History tells us that World War II was actually a continuation of the first one. It is no coincidence therefore, that Jewish people were targeted by Hitler.) The thirteenth chapter of Revelation, verses 1 through 10, was fulfilled during both World Wars. The first beast was mighty in war (Revelation 13:4). The beast of the End Times is the eighth head, coming from one of the seven, and will be a controller of finances (Revelation 13:17).

The beast of the End Times will come on the scene in the near future. He is the eighth, but he was also one of the seven (Revelation 17:11). Therefore, it would be accurate to say he was not, then yet is, or "will be" (Revelation 17:8). Germany was the seventh head whose head was wounded with the sword, then was healed, then was not. Since the end of World War II, Germany has been divided. It has not been a world power, or a threat to any nation. Revelation 13:11 says that the beast of end times had two horns like a lamb. The two horns symbol-ize East and West Germany. This beast of the End Times will cause the image of the first one to come to life, which is to try and de-stroy anything that stands for the living God.

Revival
is
coming!

When God revealed this to me, I knew that East and West Germany would one day have to reunite. But as I looked at the circumstances, I thought, "I can see this happening in about ten or twenty years, but not now." Because I had so much on my mind and was going through one of the greatest trials of my life when I received this revelation, I put it out of my mind, but kept it in my heart. I was sure that I would have plenty of time to go back later and research it and write an article about it. I never expected it would begin to come about so soon.

NOW THAT I'M SAVED...

It is no coincidence that the twelve-nation European Community is working toward a unified marketplace. According to the *Wall Street Journal* of June 28, 1989, the twelve members, which include Germany, agreed on monetary-union objectives. These objectives would lead to centralized economic decision-making and a single European currency. Because of this, leading news magazines are already saying Europe will be the place to be in the 1990's.

Here are some things to watch for:

(1) A reunited Germany dominating Europe and the European Economic Community. (This is already becoming apparent.)

(2) A bankrupt United States having to convert to the European monetary system if it wants to trade with Europe. (Think about this as you see our road signs and measuring systems being changed over to European forms.)

The next war, which we are already in, will be an economic one, and Germany is going to come out on top. Dow Chemical, one of the world's largest chemical companies, has recently announced it will no longer deal in American dollars when dealing in Europe, but will use the German mark. In the short time since I originally wrote about this, which was before East and West Germany reunited, many indicators are pointing to the decline of the United States as the leading super-power. Don't expect Neo-Nazi groups to be silenced, despite all the efforts by the present leaders to do so.

Those in the Church who claim to be the Bride of Christ, but do not follow His teaching, play the part of a harlot by committing spiritual adultery. Revival is coming, but as sure as it is, persecution is also coming. God is going to put His Church through the fire. When it comes out, it will be a purified Church which will have the glory of God on it.

This isn't written to convince anyone that this is true, because time will judge whether it is or not. But my testimony is true, and the things that have already started to come to pass will be completed shortly. These are the last days, and the coming of Jesus is near.

13

This Generation Shall Not Pass

> This generation shall not pass away, till all be fulfilled.
>
> (Luke 21:32)

When Jesus was asked what the sign would be that His return would be near, He replied:

> Take heed that ye be not deceived: for many shall come in my name, saying, I am Christ.
>
> (Luke 21:8)

In verse 9, He tells us not to be terrified when we hear of wars and commotions, for those things will come before the end. He was saying that wars and commotions would always be with us. (They have been constantly with us since the beginning of recorded history.) He also said some people would say they are the Messiah.

Although what Jesus said about the end is recorded in two other Gospels, it is in the Gospel of Luke where we find the keys to understanding the events as they will unfold, and have already happened. Jesus started telling them what the signs of the end will be in Luke 21:10:

> Nation shall rise against nation, and kingdom against kingdom.

In the present age, nation is rising against nation like never before. We are reminded daily in the workplace that we are in a world-wide economic competition. Our forefathers, as a whole, tried to follow God. Now, we are reaping the harvest from a generation that forgot God. They took prayer out of our schools and made it legal to destroy unborn children while professing to be a Christian nation. The only thing that can help the hopeless situation we see in our nation today is a revival of the Church.

When Jesus said kingdom would be against kingdom, He was also talking about the kingdom of darkness and the kingdom of God. In just the last few years there has been an explosion of satanic activity. Saturday morning children's cartoons, and Satan-promoting rock-and-roll bands are helping to lead many of our children down a path to destruction. Who do you think all of these satanic tee-shirts, that are worn by many of our young people, glorify? The tragedy of it all is that while Satan is leading millions to hell like a Pied Piper, most of the Church continues to sleep.

And great earthquakes shall be in divers places, and famines, and pestilences; and fearful sights and great signs shall there be from heaven.

(Luke 21:11)

In the past few years, there have been more major earthquakes than ever before. In recent years, we have seen storms and natural disasters hit the globe with record fury. (The Greek word that is translated as "earthquake" in the King James Version also means "turmoil of the air and ground.") The worst famines in recorded history have been plaguing Africa in the last few years. These things are just the beginning of worse things to come.

His coming is near.

The word "pestilence" is translated from a word that means "a plague." Its literal meaning is "disease." We have an outbreak of disease like the world has never seen. In the near future, we will realize just how catastrophic the results of AIDS will be.

In verse 12 of Luke 21, Jesus said there would be fearful sights and great signs in heaven. He said, "But before all these . . ." He was going to tell them of things that would happen before the end-time signs. From verse 12 to the middle of verse 24, He told them of things that were going to happen in that generation. He also foretold the destruction of Jerusalem.

In verse 20, Jesus said that when they saw Jerusalem surrounded by armies, they would know the desolation thereof was near. Matthew and Mark also tell of the same event. They refer to it as "the abomination of desolation spoken of by Daniel the prophet." Some believe this refers to the sacrifice in the Temple being taken away. But if you compare Luke 21:20, Matthew 24:15, and Mark 13:14, it is clear that all three gospel writers were speaking of the same event. The abomination of desolation was when the Roman armies sur-rounded Jerusalem and destroyed it. The key to understanding this is found in Luke 21:20. (For further insight into how terrible the desolation was, you can find reference to it in the writings of Josephus, a Jewish historian.)

As Jesus said, that generation did not pass until all He said would happen came to pass. Now we are in the time of the last generation, when "all these" things referred to in Luke 21:12, have begun to come to pass. In the same way that summer is near when the trees start to bud, now that we see all these things happening, we can be sure His coming is near.

The Roman armies would not only tread Jerusalem under their feet, but Jerusalem would be under Gentile control for about 1,900 years. This was referred to in verse 24 as "the time of the Gentiles." This is another verse that has been misinterpreted. Some believe the "times of the Gentiles" refers to a set time when the Gentiles can be saved. They further believe that after this time they cannot be saved, but only the Jews can be saved. This is not so. Rather, it refers to the time in which the Gentiles controlled Jerusalem. This time was fulfilled in 1967 when the Jews gained full control of the city. From 1948, when they gained control of half of the city, until 1967, when they gained full control of it, the other half was controlled by the Arabs. The "times of the Gentiles" has been fulfilled, because Jerusalem is no longer under their control.

In the last half of verse 24, Jesus picks up where He left off in verse 11, by telling of signs of the End Times. Here, He again starts to tell of things which would happen in the End Times. After the "times of the Gentiles" was fulfilled, Jesus said there would be signs in the sun, in the moon, and in the stars; and upon the earth there will be distress of nations, with perplexity. The sea and the waves will roar.

In verse 26, He said that men's hearts would fail them for fear, as a result of looking after those things which are coming upon the earth. We are told:

> So likewise ye, when ye see these things come to pass, know ye that the kingdom of God is nigh at hand.
>
> (Luke 21:31)

14

The Perfect Mediator

Though he were a Son, yet learned he
obedience by the things which he suffered;
And being made perfect, he became the
author of eternal salvation unto all them that
obey him.

(Hebrews 5:8-9)

It may be hard for us to understand, but the
Word says that Christ learned obedience by the
things He suffered. It was not until Jesus had
to face something that He did not desire to do
that He learned what it was to be obedient. It
was when He faced the sufferings of the Cross
that this process came to full fruition in His life.
Before this, He had always coexisted with the
Father and was in perfect agreement with Him.
It wasn't that Jesus was not in agreement with
Him about the crucifixion, rather, He simply and
understandably did not look forward to the
sufferings of the Cross.

NOW THAT I'M SAVED...

The Scriptures clearly show that Jesus did not desire to endure the sufferings of the Cross. But because it was His Father's will, He denied what He felt in His flesh and went obediently to the Cross. As a man, Jesus learned what it is to deny self and obey the will of God. The Scriptures tell us that Jesus prayed, "O my Father, if it be possible, let this cup pass from me: nevertheless not as I will, but as thou wilt" (Matthew 26:39). This was the first and only time the Son of God ever had to face doing something He did not desire to do, but He did it only because it was His Father's will. This is why the Scripture tells us that He learned obedience by the things He suffered. We must not forget, although He is the Son of God, He lived His life on earth as a man.

Jesus prayed to His Father three times, "If it be possible, let this cup pass from me: nevertheless not as I will, but as thou wilt." He even said that His soul was "exceeding sorrowful unto death" (Mark 14:34). This statement concerned what He knew He would be facing, and He was in deep prayer about this. Jesus spoke several times of "the cup" His Father had given Him to drink. Though He would have preferred that His Father's will would be fulfilled in some other way, if it were possible, He drank His Father's cup. By doing so, He learned obedience unto death, by going to the Cross. He knew there was no other way, but while he was in the flesh He had to overcome the desires of the flesh and to do God's will. The

Scriptures clearly show that Jesus was tempted in every way we are, yet He was without sin (Hebrews 4:15).

Something happened between the time when Jesus prayed in the garden of Gethsemane and the moment of His death. The Scripture shows that before He died Jesus not only accepted His death because it was His Father's will, but He actually desired to drink "this cup."

Never-theless not as I will, but as thou wilt.

> After this, Jesus know-ing that all things were now accomplished, that the scripture might be fulfilled, saith, I thirst.
> (John 19:28)

The cup that He now thirsted for was "this cup" that He had earlier prayed about to His Father. He did not make this statement in reference to a physical thirst Seeing that all things were now accomplished, He thirsted to drink the cup which His Father had set before Him.

This was quite a contrast from His agony in the garden, when He asked His Father to let "this cup" pass from Him. The cup for which He now thirsted was much more bitter than the vinegar they gave Him to drink when He was on the Cross. Before He could drink this cup of death, and have the sins of the world put upon Him, His

Father had to forsake Him. If not, He could never have died in our place as a sacrifice for our sins. Although Jesus had never done any wrong, He died on a cruel Cross, but He did that for our sins, so we could be set free from the curse of the Law. That curse is "spiritual death."

Jesus became the perfect mediator between God and man. He knows what it is like to be tempted, for He was tempted in all the ways we are tempted.

> For we have not an high priest which cannot be touched with the feeling of our infirmities; but was in all points tempted like as we are, yet without sin.
>
> (Hebrews 4:15)

He also knows what it means to deny self and be obedient to the Father, even unto death. He is God, yet He lived as a man, and although He has never sinned, He has suffered, and was also tempted like we are. By experiencing these things, He became the perfect Mediator between the Father and us (1 Timothy 2:5).

James 1:13 tells us that God cannot be tempted with evil, neither does He tempt anyone. However, when Jesus took the form of man upon Himself, He was tempted, yet without sin. Hebrews 2:9-18 tells us that Jesus was made a little lower than the angels for the suffering of death, crowned with glory and honor; that He by the grace of God, should taste death for every man. Jesus took on the form of man so He, through death, could destroy the works of the devil. He was also made like us so He could be a merciful and faithful high priest in things pertaining to God, and thereby make reconciliation for the sins of the human race. He experienced being tempted, so He can now help us who are tempted.

Jesus Christ is not only our high priest, He is the perfect high priest. He knows the heart and mind of God, for He is God, and He knows what it is to be tempted. He is now in the presence of God, the Father, making intercession for those who will accept Him as their Savior. We can come to Him boldly because we know He suffered being tempted and was Himself obedient unto death (Hebrews 4:14-16 and Philippians 2:8).

15

The Crossroads of Life

> Enter ye in at the strait gate: for wide is
> the gate, and broad is the way, that leadeth
> to destruction, and many there be which go
> in thereat: Because strait is the gate, and
> narrow is the way, which leadeth unto life,
> and few there be that find it.
>
> (Matthew 7:13-14)

A crossroads is the intersection of two roads that lead in opposite directions. As we travel along life's highway we come to many such intersections that require us to make choices about which way to go. The most important of all such intersections, however, is the one Jesus refers to in Matthew 7—at that crossroad, we find a road leading to life intersecting with a road leading to destruction. It is a crucial choice.

Many folks blindly choose the road to destruction. They are like the description given by the writer of Proverbs:

> There is a way that seemeth right unto a man, but the end thereof are the ways of death.
>
> (Proverbs 16:25)

Such folks are spiritually blind and, therefore, they have no idea that they are doomed. This is why it is so important for us to witness to others; in so doing, we may truly be giving sight to the blind.

God has opened my eyes to His ways and His truths on numerous occasions. Many times He has given me visions to help me to see the right way more clearly so that I would be able to make good choices as I journey through life. I'd like to share one of those spiritual experiences with you.

After a long time of prayer, during which I felt the presence of God very near to me, I suddenly found myself being transported out of my body. It was an experience somewhat like the one described by the apostle Paul:

> I knew a man in Christ above fourteen years ago, (whether in the body, I cannot tell; or whether out of the body, I cannot tell: God knoweth;) such an one caught up to the third heaven. And I knew such a man, (whether in the body, or out of the body, I cannot tell: God knoweth;) How that he was caught up into paradise, and heard unspeakable words, which it is not lawful for a man to utter.
>
> (2 Corinthians 12:2-4)

I don't know where I was taken, but I found myself before the ruins of a deserted building. Darkness covered the scene. Pieces of columns lay all around the front of this building and other debris was scattered in all directions.

Soon I realized there was an angel who was accompanying me on my tour. I asked him what the scene in front of me meant.

"It is your life," the glorious being answered.

In amazement and concern, I questioned him further, "Why is it so dark?"

"So that you can understand that without the light, which is Christ, there is total separation from God forever."

Thy word is a lamp unto my feet.

An intense fear gripped me. I cannot fully describe how terrible it felt; it was a sense of horror stronger than anything I had ever known.

In the midst of my panic reaction, the angel withdrew his presence from me. I was left feeling devoid of hope. There was absolutely no sense of the presence of God that I had been enjoying during my prayer time. My mind raced to the conclusion, "This is the judgment, and I am not ready!"

The intense fear turned to unbearable heat. It felt as if someone was pouring molten lead or lava over my entire body. It was not only

coursing down my body, but it was filling my
entire being with a burning sensation so severe
that I thought I would literally explode. The pain
was more than excruciating; it was like
experiencing thousands of deaths all at once. I
was totally out of control, and I felt certain that
the fear and pain would drive me insane.

Just then, a brilliantly beautiful light appeared
atop the demolished building. In the radiance I
could see that the top of the structure had been
a dome. In the manner of a solar eclipse, the light
moved from the side until it filled the dome
entirely with its glorious manifestation. Then I
remembered that the ruined building was my
life, and as the light filled its dome, I could feel
peace and love being restored to my head, my
heart, and my whole body. All the fear and pain
were gone; they simply evaporated as the light
and warmth of God flooded into me.

I never knew such wonderful feelings were
possible. God had permitted me to experience
what a lost person will feel on Judgment Day. I
knew their hopelessness, their pain, their fear,
and I realized that those feelings will be eternally
devastating to them. The heat of the fires of hell
and the loss of the presence of God are
unendurable, and yet the lost will have to endure
them forever.

The angel reappeared in order to take me to
a crossroad. The road on the right was narrow
and winding. It was littered with additional
remains from the building that represented my
life. These broken pieces were like rock walls,

obstacles too large to climb over or go around. The road had to snake its way around them. Darkness, darker than any forest, formed walls on either side of the twisting road.

In the distance, well past the obstacles, I could see a beautiful green meadow. The sky above it was filled with sunshine. The road ended there.

The road on the left was a straight and wide thoroughfare. I could see it getting wider, but darker, as it went on. There was no meadow with bright skies at its termination, however. Instead, there was pitch-darkness. The blackness it headed toward was deeper than a chunk of coal. Like the road to the right, this passageway was strewn with pieces of broken columns as well, but the road went right through them.

The angel who was guiding me said, "The road to the right is the way home." (I felt certain that he was referring to heaven.) He went on, "The columns are the things you will have to encounter in your life. It will be your responsibility to go past them." (I sensed that he was referring to the trials, tribulations, and temptations we all must face.) "After you get past these things," he explained, "it will be a straight path home." (Now I knew he meant heaven.)

At that point I found myself back in my body, but there was a big difference—I was changed forever. I could never forget what I learned. It was the most powerful experience of my life.

As months went on, God continued to reveal new things to me, by His Holy Spirit—things that helped me to understand the full meaning of the supernatural experience. He showed me that the two roads I saw that day are the ones Jesus mentioned in Matthew 7:13-14. I began to understand that even believers must face the same kinds of trials, tribulations, and temptations that people in the world face. The difference is found in the road we choose.

When Jesus talks about one road being "narrow," He is referring to it being crowded. The original word may be translated as afflicted, narrow, pressed, thronged, or suffering. It is the same root word that is translated as "afflicted" in Matthew 24:9, 2 Corinthians 1:6, 1 Timothy 5:10, and Hebrews 11:37. Elsewhere, it is translated as "trouble" or "troubled," such as in 2 Corinthians 4:8 and 7:5 and 2 Thessalonians 1:6-7. In 1 Thessalonians 3:4, it is translated as "suffer tribulation."

The only New Testament passage that translates this root word as "narrow" is in Matthew 7:14. W. E. Vine states that the word means, "hemmed in like a mountain gorge; the way is rendered narrow by the divine conditions, which make it impossible for any to enter who think the entrance depends upon self-merit, or who still incline towards sin, or desire to continue evil." This is a very appropriate interpretation, in fact, it agrees with the vision I received during my supernatural experience.

The "narrow way" is made ever more narrow by the trials and tribulations we must face in life. Conversely, for those who take a broad road, the trials and tribulations serve to make the road to destruction ever wider. In order to face the trials of life, I learned through this experience and the Word of God that we must look to Jesus Christ and His Word to show us the way. "Thy word is a lamp unto my feet, and a light unto my path" (Psalm 119:105). Jesus is the way, and He is the Word made flesh. His Word is life, and it is sharper than any two-edged sword.

The unfortunate souls who wander blindly on the dark road of destruction do not know enough to look to the Light of the world (Jesus) for the spiritual life and illumination they need. Their carnal nature leads them to look in the opposite direction. Believers and unbelievers alike have to face the same kinds of things, but they are on different roads. Each road leads to a different destination.

Paul wrote:

> For verily, when we were with you, we told you before that we should suffer tribulation; even as it came to pass, and ye know.
>
> (1 Thessalonians 3:4)

Peter explained it this way:

> Beloved, think it not strange concerning the fiery trial which is to try you, as though some strange thing happened unto you: But rejoice, inasmuch as ye are partakers of Christ's sufferings.
>
> (1 Peter 4:12-13)

NOW THAT I'M SAVED. . .

In verse 19 of the fourth chapter of 1 Peter, Peter goes on to say:

> Wherefore let them that suffer according to the will of God commit the keeping of their souls to him in well doing, as unto a faithful Creator.

The Scriptures are clear about this. We must go through certain trials and tribulations in this life, but it is also clear that we do not have to do so alone. God is faithful, and He will not permit us to go through more than we can bear.

> There hath no temptation taken you but such as is common to man: but God is faithful, who will not suffer you to be tempted above that ye are able; but will with the temptation also make a way to escape, that ye may be able to bear it.
> (1 Corinthians 10:13)

The trials we go through are common to mankind, but as we walk the narrow road, being always careful to stay on course, we will discover eternal life. God's weapons will be with us as we continue to walk toward the Promised Land. His weapons are mighty, and they will protect us and enable us to fight the good fight of faith.

> No weapon that is formed against thee shall prosper; and every tongue that shall rise against thee in judgment thou shalt condemn.
> (Isaiah 54:17)

The trials of life can become steppingstones to victory when we keep our lives on the right track after choosing the road to life. By remaining focused on Jesus, the Author and Finisher of our faith, we will persevere. It is He who enables us to "run with patience the race that is set before us" (Hebrews 12:1).

16

Drawing Near To God

> Submit yourselves therefore to God.
> Resist the devil, and he will flee from you.
> Draw nigh to God, and he will draw nigh to
> you.
>
> (James 4:7-8)

So many people are putting extraordinary effort into gaining the things of this world instead of living for Jesus Christ. It is my desire that God will use this book to help people see their need to put God first, to seek Him and His righteousness (Matthew 6:33).

As I pointed out earlier, there are two roads from which we must choose—the road to life and the road to death. This is the contrast Paul refers to when he writes:

> For to be carnally minded is death; but to
> be spiritually minded is life and peace.
>
> (Romans 8:6)

The stark contrast is further revealed in Paul's letter to the Galatians:

> Now the works of the flesh are manifest, which are these; Adultery, fornication, uncleanness, lasciviousness, Idolatry, witchcraft, hatred, variance, emulations, wrath, strife, seditions, heresies, Envyings, murders, drunkenness, revellings, and such like: . . . But the fruit of the Spirit is love, joy, peace, long-suffering, gentleness, goodness, faith, Meekness, temperance: against such there is no law.
>
> (Galatians 5:19-23)

Paul continues to paint this vivid contrast throughout his letters to the young churches. He says that those who belong to Christ have crucified their sinful natures, and he pointed out that those who are "led by the Spirit of God, they are the sons of God" (Romans 8:14).

If we follow Paul's example and teaching, we will be able to live a victorious life, dying daily to sin. Starting today, you can learn to walk in the Spirit, becoming spiritually-minded, and thereby experiencing victory in your day-to-day living.

As we study God's Word daily and spend time getting close to Him in prayer and worship, the fruit of the Spirit grows in our lives. His indwelling presence enables us to overcome the temptations that confront us. A fruit-bearing Christian is the best witness the world will ever see.

Immersing ourselves in the Word of God dresses us in His invulnerable armor. Hiding His Word in our hearts and minds will keep us from ever being deceived and it will give us protection against temptations. This kind of spiritual discipline does require some sacrifices, however, but is it ever a sacrifice to give up something that keeps us from true happiness? We need to present everything we have and are as living sacrifices to God.

Repent— ask forgiveness of your sins.

I beseech you therefore, brethren, by the mercies of God, that ye present your bodies a living sacrifice, holy, acceptable unto God, which is your reasonable service.

(Romans 12:1)

This kind of living sacrifice is accomplished, as Paul goes on to point out, by being transformed through the renewing of our minds. It happens by washing in the water of God's Word. This enables us to become "more than conquerors through him that loved us" (Romans 8:37).

The unsaved, however, cannot know such abundant living that leads to eternal life unless we show them the way. Their lot, both in this life and in the life to come, will be entirely different. Should they remain unrepentant, they will find themselves in "a lake of fire burning with brimstone" that John describes in Revelation. This was the fire I experienced as I underwent my vision-experience. It's a horror that defies description.

After my experience of hell, I was blessed by the peace of God. It's the peace that the redeemed will know in glory. It's like being wrapped in a blanket woven of God's love.

What will your choice be?

Peace and love, or chaos and confusion?

Heaven or hell?

Hope or hopelessness?

Life or death?

Trust or fear?

Joy or sadness?

Light or darkness?

> There is no fear in love; but perfect love casteth out fear: because fear hath torment. He that feareth is not made perfect in love.
> (1 John 4:18)

You can have the assurance of eternal life and know that you will be with God forever, or you can receive eternal condemnation and torment. The decision is yours alone. If you would like to accept Jesus Christ as your Savior, or if you have an opportunity to lead someone to the Lord, carefully read and follow these important steps:

Believe—you must have faith. Believe that Jesus is the Son of God and that He died for your sins (John 3:16-21; Romans 5:1-2; 1 John 5:1).

Repent—ask forgiveness of your sins (Luke 13:3; Acts 17:30; 1 John 1:9).

Confess with your mouth that Jesus Christ is your Savior (Luke 12:8-9; Romans 10:9-11; 1 John 1:8-10).

Be baptized (Acts 2:38; Romans 6:1-9; 1 Peter 3:21).

Obey—take up your cross and follow Him. Be obedient to His commandments (Matthew 10:38; Romans 2:6-13; 1 John 2:3-6).

My prayer, as I conclude this book, is that it will truly be a revelation of God's Word and will to you. May that revelation lead you to find newness of life through Jesus Christ.